CONTENTS

The Magic of Compound Interest	1
Prologue	2
Chapter 1: Introduction to Compound Interest	5
Chapter 2: The Power of Time	11
Chapter 3: The Magic of Regular Contributions	18
Chapter 4: Interest Rates and Their Impact	29
Chapter 5: The Rule of 72	40
Chapter 6: Investing in Different Financial Instruments	49
Chapter 7: Risk Management	59
Chapter 8: The Impact of Inflation	70
Chapter 9: Tax Implications	82
Chapter 10: Building a Compound Interest Plan	93
Chapter 11: Behavioural Finance	103
Chapter 12: The Role of Financial Advisors	116
Chapter 13: Technology and Investing	127
Chapter 14: Retirement Planning	139
Chapter 15: Building Wealth for Future Generations	150

Chapter 16: Conclusion	161
Epilogue	169
References	174
Legal Notice	177
Copyright Information	178
Disclaimer	179

THE MAGIC OF COMPOUND INTEREST

How To Multiply Your Money

Dr Bhaskar Bora

PROLOGUE

In the bustling heart of any city, amidst the towering skyscrapers and the hum of commerce, lies a simple yet profound truth—money, when handled with wisdom and foresight, has the potential to grow beyond our wildest dreams. This truth, often shrouded in the complex jargon of finance, is accessible to all who seek to understand it. It is the magic of compound interest.

Imagine a small seed planted in fertile soil. With time, care, and the right conditions, this seed will grow into a towering tree, bearing fruit year after year. The principle of compound interest operates in much the same way. It transforms modest savings into substantial wealth, provided one has the patience to let it grow and the wisdom to nurture it properly.

For centuries, the concept of compound interest has been the cornerstone of wealth building, silently working its magic for those who understood its power. From ancient merchants to modern-day moguls, the ability to multiply money through compound interest has been a well-guarded secret, often overshadowed by more glamorous financial strategies. Yet, its simplicity and effectiveness remain unmatched.

This book, "The Magic of Compound Interest - Multiply Your Money Now," is your gateway to unlocking this age-old secret. It is a journey through the fundamentals of compound interest, illustrated with real-life examples, practical strategies, and actionable insights. Whether you're just starting on your financial journey or looking to refine your investment strategy, this book offers valuable knowledge to help you harness the full potential of your money.

Our journey begins with understanding the essence of compound interest and its profound impact over time. We will explore the importance of starting early, regular contributions' benefits, and patience's power. You will learn about different investment vehicles, tax-efficient strategies, and the psychological aspects of investing. Together, we will build a comprehensive plan to grow wealth and secure your financial future.

But this book is more than just a guide; it is a call to action. It challenges you to take control of your financial destiny, to think long-term, and to make informed decisions. The magic of compound interest is not reserved for the elite; it is a tool for anyone willing to learn and apply its principles.

As you turn these pages, envision the life you desire—a life of financial independence, security, and opportunities for you and your loved ones. Let the power of compound interest work for you, transforming your financial dreams into reality.

Welcome to the journey of multiplying your money.

Welcome to the magic of compound interest.

CHAPTER 1: INTRODUCTION TO COMPOUND INTEREST

Understanding Compound Interest And Its Significance

Compound interest is a powerful financial concept that can grow your wealth significantly over time, unlike simple interest, which is calculated only on the initial principal, compound interest factors in both the principal and the accumulated interest from previous periods. This means you earn "interest on interest," creating a snowball effect where your money grows at an accelerating pace.

The Significance of Compound Interest

1. Exponential Growth

The main appeal of compound interest is its ability to generate exponential growth over time. As your investment earns interest, that interest starts to generate more interest. Over long periods, this results in much faster growth compared to simple interest. A small initial investment can grow into a substantial sum due to this compounding effect.

2. The Role of Time

Time is a critical factor in the effectiveness of compound interest. The earlier you start investing, the more time you give your money to compound. The longer you allow compound interest to work, the larger your investment grows. This is why financial experts always emphasise the importance of starting to save and invest as soon as possible, even with small amounts.

3. Passive Wealth Accumulation

One of the most attractive features of compound interest is its ability to accumulate wealth with minimal effort. After making an initial investment, the interest compounds without requiring continuous active management. This passive nature makes it ideal for long-term wealth building.

4. Inflation Protection

Inflation gradually reduces the purchasing power of money, meaning that over time, the same amount of money buys fewer goods and services. Compound interest helps counteract this by ensuring that your investment grows faster than inflation, preserving and even increasing the real value of your money.

5. Retirement Planning

Compound interest is essential in planning for a comfortable retirement. Regular contributions to retirement accounts, such as 401(k)s or IRAs, combined with compounding, can ensure that you have enough funds to sustain you in your later years. The longer you contribute, the more compound interest helps your retirement savings grow.

Historical Background of Compound Interest

The concept of compound interest is not new. It has been understood and applied for thousands of years. Early civilisations like the Babylonians recognised the power of compound interest and used it in their financial transactions, particularly in lending and banking. This idea of earning interest on interest was considered advanced even in ancient times.

In more recent history, prominent figures such as Albert Einstein have emphasised the importance of compound interest, with Einstein famously (though perhaps apocryphally) referring to it as the "eighth wonder of the world." This highlights the tremendous impact it can have on one's financial future.

The Renaissance period in Europe saw the development of complex financial instruments where compound interest played a pivotal role. Influential banking families, like the Medici, used it to grow their wealth and fund vast commercial enterprises. By the Industrial Revolution, the widespread use of compound interest had revolutionised business finance and personal savings.

Real-World Impact of Compound Interest

The impact of compound interest can be seen in many areas of personal finance. Let's explore some practical applications:

1. Savings Accounts

Imagine depositing $5,000 in a savings account with a modest interest rate of 2%, compounded monthly. Over 20 years, this amount would grow to over $7,500. Though the rate seems small, the compounding effect over time leads to a notable increase.

2. Retirement Savings

If you contribute $200 per month to a retirement fund with a 6% annual interest rate, compounded monthly, after 30 years, your total contributions of $72,000 would grow to about $200,000. This shows the combined power of regular contributions and compound interest over time.

3. Education Funds

Starting an education fund with $10,000, at a 4% annual interest rate compounded annually, while contributing $100 each month, would grow to over $54,000 after 18 years. This example demonstrates the importance of starting early and making regular contributions, allowing compound interest to build significant wealth.

4. Investment Portfolios

Let's consider an investor who places $50,000 into a diversified portfolio with a 7% annual return. Over 25 years, the value of the portfolio would grow to over $270,000. The longer the investment remains, the greater the impact of compound interest.

5. Debt Management

Compound interest can also work against you when it comes to debt. For example, with a credit card balance of $5,000 and a 20% annual interest rate compounded monthly, failing to pay off the balance quickly can result in substantial debt growth. Understanding compound interest is crucial in managing and avoiding high-interest debt.

Why Compound Interest Is So Powerful

1. The Snowball Effect

When you invest or save money with compound interest, the initial amount begins earning interest. As that interest is added to your balance, it, too, begins earning interest. Over time, this compounding creates a snowball effect, where your wealth grows faster and faster.

2. More Frequent Compounding

The frequency with which interest compounds is an important factor. The more often interest is compounded, the faster your money grows. For instance, daily compounding will yield greater returns than annual compounding, assuming all other factors are the same.

3. The Rule of 72

A simple way to estimate how long it will take for an investment to double is the Rule of 72. Divide 72 by the annual interest rate to get the approximate number of years it will take for your money to double. For example, at a 6% interest rate, it will take roughly 12 years for your money to double (72 / 6 = 12).

Conclusion

Compound interest is a key component of wealth building. Its ability to accelerate the growth of your investments and savings is unparalleled, and the earlier you start, the more you can benefit. From planning for retirement to funding education or managing debt, compound interest is a powerful financial tool that can either work for you or against you. By understanding its principles and applying them effectively, you can set yourself up for long-term financial success.

CHAPTER 2: THE POWER OF TIME

The Role Of Time In Compound Interest

When it comes to investing and wealth building, time plays an incredibly powerful role. The more time you allow your money to sit and grow, the more it benefits from the force of compound interest. This principle—often referred to as "time in the market"—demonstrates the value of patience and long-term thinking in investment strategies.

Unlike simple interest, where your returns are only calculated on the original amount you invest (the principal), compound interest works by calculating returns not only on your principal but also on the interest that has already been earned. This means that the interest you earn starts to generate its interest, creating a snowball effect of growth.

Let's break it down:

If you invest $1,000 today, and over time, your investment earns interest, that interest will be added to the original amount. The next time interest is calculated, it's on the larger amount—your initial investment plus the interest it's already earned. This compounding effect continues over time, causing your money to grow faster and faster. The longer you leave your money invested, the more this effect accelerates.

A great way to understand the power of time in investing is by comparing two investors:
- Investor A starts investing $200 per month at the age of 25.
- Investor B starts investing $400 per month at the age of 35.

Both investors earn an annual return of 6%, but Investor A, despite contributing less per month, will have accumulated significantly more wealth by the time they reach age 65. This happens because Investor A started ten years earlier, giving compound interest more time to work its magic. Investor B will have to contribute twice as much and still won't reach the same total.

This example makes a compelling case for starting early. Even small, consistent contributions can grow exponentially if given enough time, making early investment a powerful strategy for building long-term wealth.

Case Studies: The Long-Term Benefits of Compound Interest

Learning from real-life examples can help to visualise how time can amplify the effects of compound interest.

1. Warren Buffett's Strategy

One of the most famous investors of all time, Warren Buffett, began investing at the age of 11. His long-term approach has centred on holding shares in companies for decades, allowing compound interest to do the heavy lifting. By investing early and letting his investments sit for years, Buffett has accumulated enormous wealth, much of it after he turned 50. His story shows that success isn't about quick returns but about giving your money the time it needs to grow.

2. Retirement Funds

Regular contributions to retirement accounts like a 401(k) or IRA are another excellent example of how time and compound interest work together. If someone starts contributing to a retirement fund in their early twenties, even with modest monthly amounts, the results can be astonishing by the time they retire. Over 30 or 40 years, their money grows exponentially, ensuring a substantial nest egg for their future.

3. Education Savings

Parents who start saving for their children's education early can also leverage the power of compound interest. By contributing regularly to a 529 plan or another education savings account, they allow their money to compound over the years, potentially covering a large portion, if not all, of the education expenses. By starting when their children are young, they give themselves the best chance to accumulate the funds needed without having to make significant financial sacrifices later.

These case studies demonstrate that the most critical factor in successful investing is time. The earlier you start, the more opportunities compound interest has to grow your investment.

The Importance of Starting Early: A Detailed Look

Starting early is the single most effective way to harness the full potential of compound interest. Why? Because the earlier you begin, the more time your money has to grow. Even small, regular investments made in your twenties can lead to significant financial gains by the time you retire.

Let's explore this through a simple comparison:
- Scenario 1: Emily starts investing $100 per month at age 25 in an account earning 6% annual interest, compounded monthly.
- Scenario 2: John starts investing $200 per month at age 35 in the same type of account.

By the time they both reach age 65:
- Emily's investment will have grown substantially, despite her lower monthly contributions, because her investments had ten extra years to compound.
- John's investment, although he contributed more per month, will still be lower than Emily's because he started later, giving compound interest less time to work.

This example illustrates a critical point: when it comes to investing, time is more valuable than the amount you invest. Starting early allows you to contribute less and still achieve the same if not better, financial outcomes. The takeaway is simple: begin your investment journey as early as possible. The longer you wait, the harder it becomes to achieve the same financial goals without contributing significantly more money later on.

The Psychological Side of Investing: How Patience Fuels Success

While the mechanics of compound interest are essential to understand, successful investing also requires a disciplined, patient mindset. The psychological aspect of investing can greatly influence whether or not you fully benefit from the power of time.

1. Delayed Gratification

One of the core challenges of investing is delaying gratification. It can be tempting to spend money in the present instead of investing it in the future. However, those who understand the benefits of compound interest are willing to make short-term sacrifices for long-term rewards. By choosing to invest rather than spend, you are essentially paying yourself in the future.

2. Resisting Emotional Decisions

Markets fluctuate, and these fluctuations can stir up emotional reactions. It's common for investors to panic during market downturns, leading to impulsive decisions like selling investments too soon. However, successful investors know that staying calm and keeping a long-term perspective is key. By riding out short-term market volatility, they allow their investments to recover and grow over time.

3. Consistency and Discipline

Consistency is critical when it comes to investing. Setting up automatic contributions to your investment accounts can help ensure that you stay on track, even when other financial obligations arise. Investors who regularly contribute to their accounts, regardless of market conditions, are more likely to benefit from compound interest over time.

4. Maintaining a Long-Term Mindset

Investing with a long-term mindset means focusing on your financial goals rather than getting caught up in day-to-day market movements. This perspective helps investors avoid panic during market downturns and prevents them from withdrawing funds prematurely. The longer you leave your investments untouched, the more time compound interest has to work in your favour.

5. Educating Yourself

Understanding the principles of compound interest and how time affects your investments helps you make informed financial decisions. The more educated you are about how your money grows, the less likely you are to fall victim to common investing mistakes, such as pulling money out too early or failing to stay consistent with contributions.

Realising the Full Power of Time

The true power of compound interest lies in its ability to accelerate wealth accumulation over time. With each passing year, the compounding effect becomes more significant. It's like planting a tree: the growth starts slow, but after many years, that tree becomes enormous. The longer you leave it to grow, the larger it becomes, and the same is true with your investments.

To maximise the benefits of compound interest:
- Start early: The sooner you start, the more time your money has to grow.
- Be consistent: Regular contributions ensure that

compound interest keeps working for you.
- Be patient: Allow your money to grow without making emotional or impulsive decisions during market volatility.
- Educate yourself: Understanding how your investments work will help you stay committed to your long-term goals.

The most successful investors aren't the ones who chase the hottest trends or time the market perfectly. They are the ones who start early, invest consistently, and remain patient, allowing compound interest and time to do the heavy lifting.

Conclusion: Time Is Your Greatest Asset

In the world of investing, time is your most valuable resource. The earlier you start investing, the more you allow compound interest to work its magic. Even modest contributions, when given enough time, can lead to significant financial gains. On the flip side, delaying your investments means you miss out on the opportunity to build wealth through compound interest.

Ultimately, the key to financial success is to start early, stay consistent, and maintain a long-term perspective. Patience and time are the most important elements of investing. Whether you are saving for retirement, a major purchase, or simply building wealth, time is the one factor that can make the biggest difference. Let it work for you by starting your investment journey today, and over time, you will see the rewards compound exponentially.

CHAPTER 3: THE MAGIC OF REGULAR CONTRIBUTIONS

Investing consistently is one of the most powerful yet often overlooked strategies for growing wealth and achieving financial security. When paired with the power of compound interest, regular investments can transform modest contributions into substantial savings over time. Whether you are saving for retirement, building an emergency fund, or planning for a major financial goal, the practice of making consistent contributions plays a pivotal role in maximising your financial growth.

In this chapter, we will explore the critical importance of consistent investments, how they can help you weather market volatility, and the strategies you can use to ensure you maintain regular contributions. Additionally, we will examine real-life case studies that illustrate the power of consistency in building wealth, discuss tools that can automate your investments, and address common challenges you may face in maintaining a disciplined approach to saving.

Why Consistency Matters in Investing

1. Building Wealth Over Time

The most fundamental reason for making regular contributions is the impact of consistent growth over time. Compound interest works best when your investment amount is steadily growing. Each new contribution adds to the principal amount, meaning the base that earns interest is always increasing. As time passes, the interest earned on both your initial investment and your regular contributions compounds, leading to exponential growth. This is why even small, regular investments can accumulate into significant sums if you give them enough time to grow.

For example, if you invest $200 each month in an account that compounds annually, your consistent contributions will increase the amount earning interest, accelerating your portfolio's growth. By maintaining this habit, you are not just relying on the performance of the market; you're actively adding to the pot that will grow.

2. Smoothing Out Market Volatility

Investing regularly also helps you manage the inherent volatility of financial markets. Stock markets and other investment vehicles can fluctuate significantly over time, with prices rising and falling due to a variety of economic factors. This volatility can be unnerving for investors, particularly those who are new to the market or who focus on short-term results.

One way to mitigate the risks of market fluctuations is through a strategy known as dollar-cost averaging. By contributing a fixed amount at regular intervals, you purchase more shares when prices are low and fewer shares when prices are high. Over time, this strategy reduces the overall cost per share, helping you avoid the common pitfall of trying to time the market. Dollar-cost averaging ensures that you continue to invest consistently, regardless of market conditions, allowing you to take advantage of both high and low points in the market without emotional decision-making.

3. Forming a Savings Habit

Consistency in investing not only builds wealth but also fosters a disciplined saving habit. Like any other habit, saving becomes easier when it is done routinely. By automating your contributions, you remove the need for constant decision-making about when and how much to invest. This automation turns investing into a "set it and forget it" process, which can be especially useful for individuals who struggle with maintaining financial discipline.

Once saving becomes a habit, you'll likely find it easier to adjust your budget to accommodate your contributions. Over time, as you see your investments grow, you may even feel motivated to increase your contributions. This positive reinforcement encourages a consistent and proactive approach to building wealth.

4. Achieving Long-Term Financial Goals

Whether you're saving for retirement, purchasing a home, or funding your child's education, regular contributions help you stay on track to meet your financial goals. By breaking your savings goals into smaller, manageable contributions, you reduce the financial pressure that comes with attempting to save large sums all at once. These smaller, more frequent investments accumulate over time, helping you reach your goals without disrupting your daily finances.

For instance, saving for a home down payment may seem like a daunting task if you try to save the entire amount in a short period. However, by making regular contributions over several years, you can steadily grow your savings without feeling overwhelmed.

Key Strategies for Making Consistent Investments

1. Automate Your Contributions

Automation is one of the most effective strategies for ensuring you invest consistently. Most banks and investment platforms offer automatic transfer options, allowing you to set up recurring transfers from your checking account to your investment accounts. By scheduling these transfers, you eliminate the risk of forgetting or skipping a contribution. Automating contributions helps remove emotional or impulsive decisions from your investment process and guarantees regular investment into your portfolio.

2. Utilize Payroll Deductions

Many employers offer payroll deduction options for retirement accounts such as 401(k)s or IRAs. This allows you to contribute directly from your paycheck before the money even reaches your checking account. Payroll deductions ensure that you are consistently saving for retirement, even if you don't actively think about it. Since the contributions are made before you see your paycheck, it becomes easier to manage your day-to-day finances without being tempted to spend the money that would have gone toward your investments.

3. Budget for Investments

Budgeting is a critical part of maintaining consistent contributions. By treating your investments like any other essential monthly expense—such as rent, groceries, or utilities—you can prioritize saving for your future. Allocate a fixed amount to your investment accounts each month and make this a non-negotiable part of your financial planning.

One way to stay committed to your budget is to include your investment contributions in your monthly budgeting software or financial planning tool. This helps ensure that you don't accidentally skip a contribution or spend money allocated for investments elsewhere.

4. Increase Contributions Gradually

As your income grows, so too should your investment contributions. Whenever you receive a raise, bonus, or windfall, consider increasing the amount you invest. A good rule of thumb is to contribute at least a portion of any increase in income to your investment accounts. By steadily increasing your contributions over time, you can accelerate your wealth-building efforts without making dramatic changes to your budget.

5. Use Windfalls Wisely

Unexpected financial gains, such as tax refunds, bonuses, or inheritances, present an excellent opportunity to boost your investments. Rather than spending these windfalls, consider allocating a portion—if not all—toward your investment portfolio. Large, one-time contributions can have a significant impact when compounded over time and can help you reach your financial goals faster.

Real-Life Examples of Consistent Contributions

To illustrate the power of consistent investments, let's explore a few real-life examples and case studies that demonstrate how regular contributions can lead to significant financial growth.

1. Retirement Savings

Consider an individual who contributes $300 per month to a retirement account that earns an average annual return of 7%. Over 30 years, these regular contributions grow to approximately $350,000. Even though the individual contributed a total of $108,000 ($300 x 12 months x 30 years), the majority of their final savings comes from the growth of their investments thanks to compound interest. This demonstrates how consistent contributions, even in relatively small amounts, can lead to significant savings over time.

2. Building an Education Fund

Imagine a parent who wants to start saving for their child's college education. They begin with an initial investment of $5,000 and continue to contribute $100 monthly into a 529 plan. With an average annual return of 5%, their savings grow to over $50,000 by the time their child is ready for college. This case study highlights how starting early and contributing regularly can ease the financial burden of education costs and ensure a well-funded college account.

3. Creating an Emergency Fund

Having an emergency fund is essential for financial security. By setting aside $200 per month in a high-yield savings account with a modest 2% annual return, compounded monthly, an individual can build a sizable fund over time. After five years, their consistent contributions will grow to more than $12,500. This amount could cover unexpected expenses, such as medical emergencies or car repairs, without derailing their financial plan.

These examples emphasize the value of consistency. Whether you are saving for retirement, education, or emergency needs, regular contributions can significantly enhance your financial stability and security.

Tools and Resources to Automate Your Investments

The key to consistency is making the process as easy as possible. Fortunately, there are numerous tools and services available to automate your investments, ensuring that your contributions are both regular and reliable.

1. Robo-Advisors

Robo-advisors are automated investment platforms that manage your portfolio based on your financial goals and risk tolerance. Once you set your goals, the robo-advisor takes care of the rest, automatically allocating your contributions, rebalancing your portfolio, and reinvesting dividends. Popular robo-advisors include Betterment, Wealthfront, and SoFi, all of which make it simple to stay invested consistently.

2. Automatic Transfers

Most banks and brokerage firms offer automatic transfer options, allowing you to set up recurring transfers from your checking or savings account to your investment accounts. These transfers can be scheduled weekly, bi-weekly, or monthly, depending on your preferences. This method is particularly useful for individuals who prefer hands-off investment management.

3. Payroll Deduction Plans

Employers that offer 401(k) or IRA options typically allow employees to contribute directly from their paychecks. This form of automation ensures that you never miss a contribution, as the money is taken out before you even see your paycheck. Employer-sponsored plans often have the added benefit of matching contributions, further boosting your savings.

4. Investment Apps

Investment apps like Acorns, Stash, and Robinhood offer automated investment solutions that help you contribute consistently, even in small amounts. Some apps round up your purchases and invest the spare change, while others allow you to set up automatic transfers. These apps are designed to make investing simple, even for beginners, and help you stay on track with regular contributions.

5. Financial Planning Software

Comprehensive financial planning tools like Mint, Personal Capital, and YNAB (You Need a Budget) can help you manage your budget and track your investments. These tools allow you to set savings goals, automate contributions, and monitor your progress, all in one place. Financial planning software is an excellent way to stay organized and ensure that you consistently meet your investment goals.

Overcoming Common Challenges to Consistent Investing

Despite the clear benefits of consistent contributions, many investors struggle to maintain this habit. Below are some common challenges and strategies for overcoming them:

1. Budget Constraints

For many individuals, a tight budget can make it difficult to invest regularly. If this applies to you, start small. Even small contributions can add up over time, especially when compounded. As your financial situation improves, you can gradually increase your contributions. Prioritizing investments in your budget, even if it means starting with $50 or $100 per month, is better than waiting for the perfect time to start.

2. Market Volatility

Market fluctuations can cause anxiety, particularly for new investors. The fear of investing at the wrong time can lead to hesitation. However, remember that investing is a long-term strategy. Dollar-cost averaging helps reduce the impact of market volatility, and consistently investing through market highs and lows ensures that you don't miss out on future growth.

3. Lack of Discipline

Maintaining discipline with regular contributions can be challenging, especially when other financial demands arise. Automating your investments is an effective way to ensure you remain consistent. By setting up automatic transfers or payroll deductions, you eliminate the need for self-discipline, making investing a seamless part of your financial routine.

4. Unexpected Expenses

Unexpected expenses, such as medical bills or car repairs, can disrupt your investment plan. To prevent this, build an emergency fund that can cover 3 to 6 months of living expenses. Having this financial cushion allows you to handle unexpected costs without interrupting your regular contributions to your investments.

5. Lack of Knowledge

For some, a lack of knowledge about investing can create hesitation and prevent them from making regular contributions. Take the time to educate yourself on the basics of investing, compound interest, and the importance of long-term growth. The more informed you are, the more confident you will feel about making consistent investments.

Conclusion: The Long-Term Benefits of Consistent Investing

The importance of consistent investments cannot be overstated. By regularly contributing to your investment accounts, you harness the power of compound interest, smooth out market volatility, and build wealth over time. Consistency is the foundation of any successful investment strategy, providing the discipline and structure needed to achieve long-term financial goals.

Whether you are saving for retirement, building an emergency fund, or planning for a major purchase, regular contributions are key to achieving financial stability. By automating your contributions, leveraging tools that simplify the investment process, and addressing the challenges that may arise, you can set yourself on the path to financial success.

Remember, investing is a marathon, not a sprint. The sooner you start and the more consistently you invest, the greater your financial rewards will be. Make consistent contributions a cornerstone of your financial plan and let time and compound interest work their magic in building your wealth.

CHAPTER 4: INTEREST RATES AND THEIR IMPACT

Interest rates play a crucial role in the financial world, influencing everything from individual investments to global economies. For investors, understanding how interest rates work and how they affect the growth of investments is essential for making informed decisions. The relationship between interest rates and compound interest is particularly important, as it directly impacts the returns on your savings and investments. Whether you are new to investing or an experienced financial planner, grasping the nuances of interest rates can help you make better financial choices that align with your goals.

In this chapter, we will explore the nature of interest rates, how they interact with compound interest, and the broader economic factors that influence rate movements. We will also examine historical trends, effective strategies for maximizing interest rates, and the associated risks. The aim is to provide a comprehensive understanding of how interest rates impact financial growth and how you can use this knowledge to your advantage.

Understanding Interest Rates

Interest rates are essentially the price of borrowing money or the reward for saving and investing. In simple terms, they are expressed as a percentage of the principal —the original amount of money invested or loaned. For example, if you save $1,000 in a bank account that offers an interest rate of 3%, you will earn 3% of that amount over a specific period, usually a year.

Interest rates vary depending on factors such as market conditions, government policies, and the risk associated with the borrower or investment. Higher-risk investments typically offer higher interest rates to compensate investors for the increased risk, while safer investments, such as government bonds or savings accounts, usually come with lower rates.

Types of Interest Rates

1. Fixed Interest Rates:
Fixed interest rates remain constant for the duration of the investment or loan. For example, if you invest in a certificate of deposit (CD) with a fixed interest rate, you will earn the same rate for the entire term, regardless of market changes. Fixed rates are predictable and stable, making them ideal for long-term financial planning, especially for conservative investors who prefer lower risk.

2. Variable Interest Rates:

Variable interest rates fluctuate based on changes in the market or benchmark interest rates set by central banks. These rates may increase or decrease over time, depending on economic conditions. Variable rates can offer higher returns when rates are rising, but they also come with more risk, as rates may fall, reducing your potential earnings.

Factors That Influence Interest Rates

Several factors influence interest rates, including:

- Inflation: Central banks often raise interest rates to combat high inflation. Higher rates discourage borrowing and spending, which can help reduce inflation. Conversely, during periods of low inflation, central banks may lower rates to encourage borrowing and stimulate economic growth.

- Economic Growth: In a growing economy, interest rates tend to rise as businesses seek capital to expand, and consumers are more willing to borrow. During economic downturns, interest rates are usually lowered to encourage spending and investment.

- Central Bank Policies: Institutions like the Federal Reserve in the U.S. or the European Central Bank set benchmark interest rates to influence the broader economy. These rates impact everything from mortgage rates to savings account returns.

- Supply and Demand for Credit: The availability of credit and the demand for loans also affect interest rates. When demand for loans is high, interest rates may rise. Conversely, if there is an oversupply of credit, interest rates may decrease to attract borrowers.

How Interest Rates Affect Compound Interest

Compound interest is the interest calculated not only on the initial principal but also on the accumulated interest from previous periods. It's a powerful tool for building wealth because the longer your money stays invested, the more it grows exponentially over time. The interest earned in one period is added to the principal, and in the next period, you earn interest on the new, larger amount. This compounding effect becomes more pronounced over time, especially at higher interest rates.

The relationship between interest rates and compound interest is straightforward: the higher the interest rate, the faster your money will grow. However, even with lower interest rates, compound interest can still yield significant returns, particularly over long periods.

Different Interest Rate Scenarios:

1. Low Interest Rates:
   Even with low interest rates, your investments can still grow steadily through compound interest. For example, a savings account with a modest 2% interest rate, compounded monthly, will still provide consistent growth over time, although the pace may be slower. Low interest rates are typically seen in low-risk investments, such as savings accounts or government bonds.

2. Moderate Interest Rates:
   Moderate interest rates, often in the range of 5-7%, are typically seen in more diversified investment portfolios, such as a combination of stocks and bonds. These rates offer a balance between growth and stability, making them attractive for long-term investors seeking solid

returns without excessive risk.

3. High Interest Rates:
High interest rates can lead to rapid investment growth, but they often come with higher risk. Investments with high rates, such as certain high-yield bonds or real estate ventures, offer the potential for significant returns but are also subject to greater volatility. While the prospect of fast growth is enticing, it's essential to weigh the risks carefully.

Understanding how different interest rates impact your investments will help you choose the best strategy for your financial goals. A portfolio with a mix of investments—ranging from low to high interest rates—can help you achieve balanced growth.

Historical Trends in Interest Rates

Interest rates have fluctuated significantly over time, shaped by various economic, political, and global events. Looking at historical trends can provide valuable insights into how interest rates may evolve in the future and how you can adjust your investment strategies accordingly.

Key Historical Periods:

1. Early 20th Century:
Interest rates during the early 1900s were relatively stable, reflecting a period of economic growth and industrial expansion. The rates were moderate, providing steady returns on investments and loans.

2. Post-World War II Era:
The post-war economic boom in the 1950s and 1960s led to higher interest rates as the demand for capital

increased. Governments and businesses sought loans to rebuild and expand, driving up interest rates. This period saw robust economic growth and relatively high returns for investors.

3. 1970s and 1980s – The Era of High Inflation:

The 1970s were marked by high inflation, partly driven by rising oil prices and geopolitical instability. To combat inflation, central banks raised interest rates significantly, leading to some of the highest rates in modern history during the early 1980s. While these high rates made borrowing costly, they also provided substantial returns for savers and investors, especially in fixed-income securities.

4. 1990s to Early 2000s:

Interest rates generally declined from the 1990s onwards, as inflation stabilized and central banks adopted more conservative monetary policies. The dot-com boom of the late 1990s saw a surge in stock market investments, with relatively low interest rates encouraging consumer spending and corporate investment.

5. Post-2008 Financial Crisis and the COVID-19 Pandemic:

Following the 2008 financial crisis, central banks around the world slashed interest rates to near-zero levels to stimulate economic recovery. This period of historically low interest rates continued through the 2010s and was further extended in response to the COVID-19 pandemic. These low rates have made it more difficult for savers to earn substantial returns through traditional savings accounts, leading many to seek alternative investment opportunities.

What These Trends Teach Us:

The history of interest rates shows how economic conditions and central bank policies can drastically alter the financial landscape. Understanding these trends can help investors anticipate future rate movements and adapt their strategies. For example, during periods of low interest rates, investors may need to look beyond traditional savings accounts to achieve their desired returns, while periods of high interest rates may offer more opportunities for secure investments like bonds.

Strategies for Maximizing Interest Rates

Maximizing the returns on your investments often involves seeking the best possible interest rates. While you may not always have control over market conditions, there are several strategies you can use to ensure you're getting the most out of your money.

1. Diversify Your Investments:

One of the most effective ways to achieve higher returns is to diversify your portfolio. By spreading your investments across different asset classes—such as stocks, bonds, real estate, and mutual funds—you reduce the risk associated with any single investment while increasing your chances of earning higher returns. Diversification also helps you capture the benefits of different interest rates across various markets.

2. Seek Higher-Yield Investments:

Some investments naturally offer higher interest rates or returns. For example, dividend-paying stocks, corporate bonds, and real estate investment trusts (REITs) often provide higher yields than savings accounts or government bonds. However, these investments typically come with more risk, so it's essential to balance your portfolio according to your risk tolerance and financial goals.

3. Utilize Tax-Advantaged Accounts:

Tax-advantaged accounts, such as 401(k)s, IRAs, and Health Savings Accounts (HSAs), allow you to grow your investments without paying taxes on the interest earned until you withdraw the funds. These tax benefits can significantly enhance your overall returns, especially over long periods. By maximizing contributions to these accounts, you can take full advantage of compound interest without the burden of annual taxes.

4. Stay Informed About Market Trends:

Keeping up to date with financial news and market trends is essential for making informed investment decisions. Interest rates can change quickly based on economic conditions, and staying informed allows you to adjust your strategy accordingly. For example, during periods of rising interest rates, it may be beneficial to invest in short-term bonds or other assets that adjust to changing rates.

5. Consider Long-Term Investments:

Long-term investments, such as stocks and real estate, tend to offer

higher returns compared to short-term investments. While these asset classes come with more risk and volatility, they also provide greater potential for growth through compound interest. By staying invested over the long term, you allow your investments to ride out short-term market fluctuations and benefit from overall market growth.

Risks and Considerations

While higher interest rates can lead to greater returns, they also come with increased risks. It's important to understand these risks and take them into account when making investment decisions.

1. Market Volatility:

Higher-yield investments, such as stocks and real estate, are often subject to significant market volatility. While they can offer substantial returns during periods of growth, they are also more likely to experience losses during economic downturns. Diversifying your portfolio can help mitigate the impact of market swings.

2. Inflation Risk:

Inflation can erode the real value of your returns, particularly in low-interest investments. For example, if your savings account earns 2% annually, but inflation is 3%, your purchasing power is effectively decreasing. To protect against inflation, consider investments that typically outpace inflation, such as stocks or inflation-protected bonds.

3. Interest Rate Risk:

Interest rate risk is particularly relevant for bond investors. When interest rates rise, the value of existing bonds tends to fall because newer bonds offer higher rates. Conversely, when interest rates decline, bond prices typically rise. Investors in fixed-income securities should be aware of this risk and consider diversifying their holdings.

4. Credit Risk:

Credit risk refers to the possibility that a borrower or bond issuer may default on their obligations. Higher-yield investments, such as corporate bonds, often carry higher credit risk compared to government bonds or blue-chip stocks. It's essential to assess the creditworthiness of the issuer before making an investment decision.

5. Liquidity Risk:

Some higher-yield investments, such as real estate, may have lower liquidity, meaning it can take time to sell the asset or access your funds. This can be problematic if you need to access your money quickly. Make sure your investment portfolio includes a mix of liquid and illiquid assets to ensure you can meet short-term financial needs.

6. Diversification:

Diversification is key to managing risk in your investment portfolio. By spreading your investments across different asset classes, sectors, and geographic regions, you reduce the likelihood that a single poor-performing investment will significantly impact your overall returns.

Conclusion: Navigating Interest Rates for Long-Term Success

Interest rates are a powerful factor in shaping the growth of your investments, and understanding their impact is essential for long-term financial success. Whether rates are high, low, or fluctuating, the key is to stay informed and adapt your investment strategy accordingly. By diversifying your portfolio, seeking higher-yield opportunities, and utilizing tax-advantaged accounts, you can maximize the benefits of compound interest and achieve your financial goals.

At the same time, it's important to remain aware of the risks associated with higher interest rates and market volatility. Balancing risk and reward through thoughtful diversification and strategic planning will help you navigate interest rate fluctuations and build a secure financial future. Ultimately, the key to success lies in understanding how interest rates interact with your investments and using that knowledge to make informed decisions that align with your long-term objectives.

CHAPTER 5: THE RULE OF 72

A Simplified Approach To Understanding Investment Growth

The Rule of 72 is an incredibly useful and straightforward tool that helps investors estimate how long it will take for their investments to double, given a specific interest rate. While many investment calculations can involve complex mathematical formulas, the Rule of 72 provides an easy, back-of-the-envelope method for understanding the power of compound interest. In this chapter, we will dive into the Rule of 72, explore its practical applications, analyze examples of its use, discuss its limitations, and demonstrate how it can be a valuable tool in financial planning.

Understanding the Rule of 72

The Rule of 72 is a basic financial concept that allows

you to quickly estimate how many years it will take for an investment to double in value, based on its annual interest rate. The formula behind the Rule of 72 is simple: you divide the number 72 by the annual interest rate (expressed as a percentage) to determine the approximate number of years required for the investment to double.

This tool is widely used because it provides a quick estimate without needing to delve into detailed calculations. The Rule of 72 is most accurate for interest rates that fall between 4% and 10%, but even outside of this range, it remains a useful approximation.

For example:
- If your investment earns 6% per year, dividing 72 by 6 tells you that it will take roughly 12 years for your money to double.
- If you are earning 8% annually, dividing 72 by 8 gives you 9 years for your investment to double.

By understanding this simple formula, you can quickly assess the impact of different interest rates on your investment growth.

Practical Applications of the Rule of 72

The Rule of 72 is not just a theoretical tool—it has practical uses in various financial scenarios. Here are some keyways this rule can help investors and savers make informed decisions:

1. Investment Planning
   The Rule of 72 is invaluable when setting investment goals. By using it, you can estimate how long it will take to reach specific financial milestones. If, for example, you want to double your savings in 15 years, the Rule of 72

helps you determine the interest rate you'll need. Simply divide 72 by 15, and you'll know that an interest rate of approximately 4.8% will help you achieve that goal.

2. Comparing Investment Options

When faced with different investment choices, the Rule of 72 allows you to make quick comparisons. If one investment offers a 5% annual return and another offers 7%, you can use the rule to estimate how much faster the higher-yielding investment will double your money. By calculating that it will take about 14.4 years to double your money at 5% (72/5), versus 10.3 years at 7% (72/7), you can weigh the benefits of each option.

3. Understanding the Impact of Fees

Fees and expenses are a significant drag on investment returns. If a fund charges a 2% annual fee and reduces your effective interest rate from 8% to 6%, the Rule of 72 shows how much longer it will take for your money to double. With an 8% return, your money doubles in approximately 9 years, but with the 6% return (after fees), it will take 12 years. This simple calculation can help highlight the importance of choosing low-cost investment options.

4. Accounting for Inflation

Inflation erodes the purchasing power of money over time, and the Rule of 72 can be applied to understand how quickly inflation can reduce the value of your savings. For instance, if inflation averages 3% per year, the Rule of 72 tells us that the purchasing power of your money will halve in approximately 24 years (72/3). This insight emphasizes the need for investment returns that outpace inflation to preserve your wealth.

5. Evaluating Interest on Debt

The Rule of 72 can also be used to assess the impact of interest on debt. For example, if you have a credit card with an 18% annual interest rate, the Rule of 72 indicates that your debt could double in just 4 years (72/18) if you don't make payments. This realization can prompt quicker action to pay down high-interest debt and avoid letting it spiral out of control.

By using the Rule of 72 in these practical scenarios, you gain a clear sense of how interest rates—whether they apply to investments, inflation, or debt—can impact your financial situation over time.

Examples of the Rule of 72 in Action

To help illustrate the power and versatility of the Rule of 72, let's explore a few real-world examples:

1. Doubling an Investment

Suppose you invest $10,000 in a mutual fund that provides an annual return of 8%. Using the Rule of 72, you divide 72 by 8, giving you 9 years as the time it will take for your investment to double. In this case, your $10,000 would grow to approximately $20,000 after 9 years. If you leave the investment to compound further, it could double again in another 9 years, reaching $40,000.

2. Comparing Investment Returns

Imagine you are choosing between two different savings accounts. One offers a 5% annual return, and the other provides 7%. Using the Rule of 72, you can quickly determine that the first account will double your investment in 14.4 years (72/5), while the second will double it in 10.3 years (72/7). Over time, the difference in the speed of growth becomes significant, highlighting the importance of seeking higher returns when possible.

3. Accounting for Inflation

Suppose inflation is expected to average 3% annually. You can use the Rule of 72 to estimate that the purchasing power of your savings will be cut in half in roughly 24 years (72/3). This illustrates how inflation quietly erodes wealth over time and why it's important to invest in assets that grow faster than inflation.

4. Evaluating the Impact of Fees

You are considering two investment funds. Fund A charges no fees and offers a 6% annual return, while Fund B charges 1% in fees, leaving you with a net return of 5%. The Rule of 72 tells you that Fund A will double your money in 12 years (72/6), while Fund B will take 14.4 years (72/5) to achieve the same result. Over time, this seemingly small difference can have a significant impact on your investment's performance.

These examples show how versatile and valuable the Rule of 72 can be in helping you make quick, informed decisions about various financial scenarios.

Limitations of the Rule of 72

While the Rule of 72 is a powerful tool, it's important to understand its limitations. Like any simplified model, it has certain constraints that can impact its accuracy in specific situations.

1. Accuracy Across Different Interest Rates

The Rule of 72 is most accurate when dealing with interest rates between 4% and 10%. Outside this range, the estimates become less precise. For example, at very high interest rates (above 20%), the Rule of 72 tends to underestimate the time required for doubling. Similarly, at very low interest rates (below 2%), the rule may not provide accurate results.

2. Compounding Frequency

The Rule of 72 assumes that interest is compounded annually. However, many investments compound more frequently—monthly, quarterly, or daily. If your investment compounds more frequently, it may double faster than the Rule of 72 predicts. For example, a savings account that compounds interest monthly will grow more quickly than one that compounds annually, even if both offer the same nominal interest rate.

3. Impact of Taxes and Inflation

The Rule of 72 does not account for taxes and inflation, both of which can significantly affect your real returns. Taxes can reduce your effective interest rate, while inflation erodes the purchasing power of your investment. It's important to consider these factors when using the Rule of 72, especially when planning for long-term goals like retirement.

4. Variable Interest Rates

The Rule of 72 assumes a constant interest rate throughout the investment period. However, many investments, such as stocks or bonds, have fluctuating interest rates. In these cases, the Rule of 72 provides only a rough approximation. For more accurate calculations, you would need to account for the variability in returns over time.

5. Ignoring Fees and Expenses

Many investment vehicles, such as mutual funds or

retirement accounts, charge fees that can reduce your overall returns. The Rule of 72 does not factor in these costs, so it's important to subtract fees from your expected interest rate when applying the rule. Even seemingly small fees can significantly impact the time it takes for your investment to double.

Despite these limitations, the Rule of 72 remains an invaluable tool for making quick, ballpark estimates of investment growth. By keeping its constraints in mind, you can use the rule effectively without expecting it to provide perfect precision.

Using the Rule of 72 for Financial Planning

Incorporating the Rule of 72 into your broader financial planning can help you set realistic goals, make informed investment choices, and understand the long-term impact of your financial decisions. Here are a few ways you can apply the Rule of 72 in your planning:

1. Setting Financial Goals

Whether you're saving for retirement, a down payment on a house, or your child's education, the Rule of 72 can help you estimate how long it will take to achieve your goals. For example, if you need to double your retirement savings in 15 years and expect a 5% return, the Rule of 72 shows that this timeline is realistic. If the timeline seems too long, you can adjust your contributions or seek investments with higher returns.

2. Comparing Investment Options

When evaluating different types of investments—such as stocks, bonds, or mutual funds—the Rule of 72 allows you to quickly compare how long it will take for each option to double your money. By considering the interest rates offered by each option, you can choose investments that align with your risk tolerance and time horizon.

3. Understanding Fees and Costs

Investment fees can have a profound impact on your returns over time. The Rule of 72 helps you see how even small fees can extend the time it takes to reach your goals. For example, if you're considering two mutual funds with slightly different fee structures, using the Rule of 72 to calculate the impact of those fees can help you make a more informed choice.

4. Planning for Inflation

Inflation is an ever-present force that reduces the purchasing power of your money over time. By using the Rule of 72 to estimate how long it will take for inflation to erode half the value of your money, you can better plan for long-term expenses. This knowledge can guide your investment strategy, pushing you to focus on growth-oriented investments that outpace inflation.

5. Retirement Planning

For long-term goals like retirement, the Rule of 72 can be a valuable tool for estimating how your investments will grow over time. By considering different interest rates and compounding periods, you can develop a realistic retirement savings plan. For instance, if you're aiming to double your retirement savings in 10 years, the Rule of 72 can show you what kind of returns you'll need to achieve that goal.

By applying the Rule of 72 to these financial planning scenarios, you can gain greater clarity about how your money will grow over time and make more strategic investment decisions.

Conclusion: The Rule of 72 as a Guide to Financial Success

The Rule of 72 is a powerful yet simple tool that makes the complex world of compound interest easier to understand. By providing a quick way to estimate how long it will take for your investments to double, it offers valuable insights into the effects of different interest rates, fees, and inflation. While it's not a perfect tool and has its limitations, the Rule of 72 is an excellent starting point for anyone looking to gain a deeper understanding of how their investments will grow over time.

Incorporating the Rule of 72 into your financial planning can help you set realistic goals, compare investment options, and make informed decisions about your future. By understanding how the rule works and using it alongside more detailed financial analysis, you can harness the power of compound interest to build wealth and achieve your long-term financial objectives.

CHAPTER 6: INVESTING IN DIFFERENT FINANCIAL INSTRUMENTS

Investing is a key strategy for building wealth and securing your financial future, and there are various financial instruments available that cater to different risk tolerances, goals, and timelines. Each of these instruments has its own characteristics, benefits, and risks. In this chapter, we will explore some of the most common types of financial instruments—stocks, bonds, mutual funds, real estate, and cryptocurrencies—and how you can use them to grow your investments. We will also discuss how these assets benefit from the power of compound interest and long-term growth.

1. Stocks

Stocks represent ownership in a company, and when you buy shares, you are essentially buying a piece of that company. Stocks are one of the most well-known and widely used financial instruments for long-term wealth accumulation.

Key Aspects of Stock Investing

1. Understanding Stocks:

Stocks, also referred to as equities, represent partial ownership in a company. When you buy a stock, you become a shareholder, meaning you own a small portion of the company and are entitled to a share of the company's profits, which may come in the form of dividends.

2. Growth Potential:

Stocks have historically offered high potential for growth. The value of a stock can rise as a company grows or improves its performance, and over the long term, stock markets have generally provided strong returns. While annual returns fluctuate, over time, the stock market has yielded average returns of around 7-10% per year, which makes stocks a great tool for building wealth.

3. Risk and Volatility:

Investing in stocks involves a certain level of risk. Stock prices can be volatile, affected by factors such as company performance, economic trends, political events, and global markets. Because of this, stock values can rise and fall dramatically in the short term. However, for investors with a long-term horizon, this volatility can often smooth out, leading to potential gains.

4. Dividends:

Many companies distribute part of their earnings to shareholders in the form of dividends. Reinvesting dividends by purchasing more shares can amplify the benefits of compounding. This allows your investments to grow even faster as the dividends generate additional income, which then earns dividends itself.

5. Diversification:

One of the most effective ways to reduce the risk of investing in stocks is by diversifying your portfolio. Instead of investing all your money in one company or sector, spreading your investments across various companies, industries, and even countries helps to mitigate risk. Many investors use mutual funds or exchange-traded funds (ETFs) to achieve this kind of diversification.

2. Bonds

Bonds are a more conservative investment compared to stocks. They offer lower returns but come with lower risk, making them an essential part of a balanced investment portfolio.

Key Aspects of Bond Investing

1. Understanding Bonds:

Bonds are essentially loans that you give to governments, corporations, or municipalities. In exchange for your loan, the issuer agrees to pay you periodic interest payments (also known as the coupon) and return the principal (the initial investment) at the bond's maturity date. Bonds are considered fixed-income securities because they offer predictable interest payments.

2. Types of Bonds:
 - Government Bonds: Issued by national governments and typically considered the safest type of bond.
 - Municipal Bonds: Issued by local or state governments to fund public projects like schools or highways. They often offer tax advantages.
 - Corporate Bonds: Issued by companies to raise capital. These bonds offer higher yields than government bonds but carry more risk.
 - High-Yield Bonds (Junk Bonds): These offer higher returns but come with a greater risk of default, as they are issued by companies or entities with lower credit ratings.

3. Interest Payments and Stability:
Bonds provide a steady income stream through regular interest payments, which can be reinvested for compounding growth. Bonds are generally more stable than stocks, offering predictable returns and lower volatility. However, the trade-off is that bonds typically offer lower returns than stocks.

4. Risk and Return:
While bonds are considered safer than stocks, they are not entirely risk-free. The risk associated with bonds primarily depends on the creditworthiness of the issuer. Government bonds are considered the least risky, while corporate and high-yield bonds carry higher risks.

5. Diversification and Balance:
Including bonds in your portfolio can help balance the risks of stock investments. By diversifying across both stocks and bonds, you can reduce the overall volatility of

your portfolio while still capturing steady returns.

3. Mutual Funds

Mutual funds are a convenient way for investors to pool their money and gain access to a diversified portfolio of stocks, bonds, or other securities. They are professionally managed, making them an attractive option for investors who prefer a hands-off approach.

Key Aspects of Mutual Fund Investing

1. Understanding Mutual Funds:
   Mutual funds pool money from multiple investors to invest in a variety of securities, such as stocks, bonds, and other assets. Each investor owns shares of the mutual fund, representing a portion of the holdings. These funds are managed by professional portfolio managers who make decisions on behalf of the investors.

2. Types of Mutual Funds:
   - Equity Funds: Invest primarily in stocks. These funds are suited for investors seeking growth but willing to accept more risk.
   - Bond Funds: Focus on bonds, offering steady income and lower risk.
   - Balanced Funds: Invest in both stocks and bonds to balance risk and reward.
   - Index Funds: Track a specific market index, like the S&P 500. These funds typically have lower fees because they are passively managed.

3. Diversification:
   Mutual funds offer built-in diversification, as they hold a wide range of securities. This helps reduce the risk associated with any one stock or bond underperforming.

With a mutual fund, even small investors can achieve a diversified portfolio.

4. Professional Management:

Mutual funds are managed by experienced professionals who research and select the fund's investments. This active management is appealing to investors who lack the time or expertise to manage their own portfolios.

5. Fees and Expenses:

One downside to mutual funds is the fees associated with them. These can include management fees, administrative fees, and sales charges. These costs can eat into your returns, so it's important to understand the fees before investing in a mutual fund.

4. Real Estate

Real estate investing involves purchasing property with the goal of earning rental income or profiting from appreciation over time. Real estate is a tangible asset, providing both income and the potential for long-term growth.

Key Aspects of Real Estate Investing

1. Understanding Real Estate Investments:

Real estate investing can take many forms, including buying residential properties (homes, apartments), commercial properties (offices, warehouses), or investing in real estate investment trusts (REITs). REITs allow investors to gain exposure to real estate without owning physical properties.

2. Income Generation:

Rental properties provide a steady stream of income through rent payments. This income can be reinvested to purchase additional properties or invested in other financial instruments, benefiting from the compounding effect over time.

3. Appreciation:

Over time, real estate tends to appreciate in value, meaning that the property can be sold for more than its original purchase price. This capital appreciation, combined with rental income, can lead to significant returns.

4. Leverage:

One of the unique aspects of real estate is the ability to use leverage. Most investors use mortgages to finance property purchases, allowing them to control a larger asset with a smaller initial investment. Leverage amplifies returns but also increases risk, as market downturns can lead to losses.

5. Diversification and Risks:

Real estate offers diversification beyond traditional stocks and bonds, often moving independently of stock market fluctuations. However, it comes with risks, including property maintenance costs, tenant vacancies, and changes in market conditions.

5. Cryptocurrencies

Cryptocurrencies have emerged as a new and highly volatile asset class, offering both the potential for high returns and significant risks. These digital currencies are based on blockchain technology and are decentralized, making them an attractive option for investors seeking to diversify into alternative assets.

Key Aspects of Cryptocurrency Investing

1. Understanding Cryptocurrencies:
Cryptocurrencies, such as Bitcoin and Ethereum, are digital assets that use cryptography for security. They operate on decentralized networks known as blockchains. Unlike traditional currencies, cryptocurrencies are not controlled by governments or central banks.

2. Potential for High Returns:
Cryptocurrencies are known for their dramatic price swings, which can lead to both large gains and significant losses. Early investors in Bitcoin, for instance, saw substantial returns as the value of the currency skyrocketed. However, this volatility means that cryptocurrencies are a high-risk investment.

3. Risk and Volatility:
Cryptocurrencies are highly speculative and can be affected by factors like regulatory changes, technological advancements, and market sentiment. This extreme volatility can result in rapid price increases as well as sharp declines, making cryptocurrencies one of the riskiest asset classes.

4. Diversification:
For investors with a higher risk tolerance, cryptocurrencies can serve as a way to diversify beyond traditional financial markets. However, it's crucial to limit exposure to cryptocurrencies to a small portion of your overall portfolio due to their unpredictable nature.

5. Long-Term Potential:

Some investors believe that cryptocurrencies represent the future of money and have long-term growth potential. While the technology behind cryptocurrencies continues to evolve, it's important to approach these investments with caution and stay informed about market developments.

6. Security and Regulation:

Cryptocurrencies face challenges related to security, including the

risk of hacking and fraud. Moreover, the regulatory environment surrounding cryptocurrencies is still developing, and new laws can have a significant impact on the market.

Conclusion: Building a Diversified Investment Portfolio

Investing in different financial instruments allows you to spread risk while taking advantage of growth opportunities across various markets. Each asset class —stocks, bonds, mutual funds, real estate, and cryptocurrencies—offers unique benefits and risks. By understanding these financial instruments and how they can work together in a diversified portfolio, you can build a more stable investment strategy that aligns with your financial goals and risk tolerance.

The key to successful investing is not to rely on one asset class but to combine different instruments to create a balanced portfolio. This diversification helps protect against the volatility of any one market while positioning you to benefit from compound interest and long-term growth. By making informed decisions and regularly reviewing your portfolio, you can harness the power of these financial instruments to secure a strong financial future.

CHAPTER 7: RISK MANAGEMENT

Safeguarding Your Investments For Long-Term Success

Risk management is a cornerstone of successful investing, as it helps investors navigate uncertainty while pursuing financial growth. Every investment carries some level of risk, whether it's market fluctuations, economic downturns, or changes in interest rates. Understanding how to identify, assess, and manage these risks is crucial for achieving your financial goals while minimizing potential losses.

In this chapter, we will delve into the various types of investment risks, explore strategies to manage them, and examine the importance of balancing risk and reward. We'll also look at diversification techniques, essential tools for mitigating risk, and real-life case studies that highlight the importance of managing risk effectively.

Understanding Risk in Investing

Risk is inherent in investing. It's the uncertainty that comes with the possibility of losing part or all of your investment. While risk cannot be eliminated entirely, it can be managed in ways that reduce its impact. Understanding the types of risks you may face is the first step in effective risk management.

Key Types of Investment Risk

1. Market Risk:

This is the risk of losing money due to changes in the overall market. Stocks, bonds, and other assets are often affected by broad economic events, such as recessions, political instability, or global crises. Market risk, also known as systematic risk, is something that all investors face and cannot be avoided entirely.

2. Credit Risk:

Credit risk, particularly relevant for bondholders, refers to the possibility that the issuer of a bond (such as a corporation or government) may default on its payments. If the issuer fails to make interest or principal payments, the investor could suffer losses.

3. Interest Rate Risk:

This risk is related to the fluctuation of interest rates. For bond investors, rising interest rates can reduce the value of existing bonds. Conversely, falling rates can increase bond prices but may also reduce the return on future fixed-income investments.

4. Inflation Risk:

Inflation erodes the purchasing power of your money. If your investment returns don't keep pace with inflation, the real value of your gains diminishes over time. Inflation risk is especially important for long-term investments in low-yield assets like bonds or savings accounts.

5. Liquidity Risk:

Liquidity risk occurs when you are unable to sell an asset quickly without significantly lowering its price. This is more common in real estate, private equity, or niche investments. In contrast, stocks and bonds are typically more liquid and can be sold quickly at market price.

Risk Tolerance

Your risk tolerance is a personal measure of how much volatility you can endure in your investment portfolio. It's a combination of your financial situation, investment goals, and emotional response to risk. For example, younger investors with longer time horizons can often tolerate more risk because they have time to recover from market downturns. In contrast, those nearing retirement might prefer more conservative investments to preserve their capital.

Risk vs. Reward

There is a clear trade-off between risk and reward in investing. Typically, higher-risk investments offer the potential for higher returns, but they also come with a greater chance of loss. Conversely, lower-risk investments tend to provide more stability but often generate lower returns. Managing this trade-off effectively is key to building a portfolio that aligns with your financial goals.

Asset Allocation

Asset allocation refers to the strategy of dividing your investments among different asset classes, such as stocks, bonds, and real estate, based on your risk tolerance and financial goals. A well-balanced asset allocation plan helps spread risk and ensures that your portfolio is diversified enough to weather different market conditions. Over time, rebalancing your portfolio to maintain your desired allocation can also help manage risk.

Diversification Strategies for Risk Management

Diversification is one of the most effective risk management strategies. By spreading your investments across different asset classes, sectors, and geographical regions, you reduce the impact of any single investment's poor performance on your overall portfolio.

Key Diversification Strategies

1. Asset Class Diversification:

The simplest form of diversification is investing in multiple asset classes, such as stocks, bonds, real estate, and cash. Each asset class behaves differently under various market conditions, and by holding a mix of these assets, you can reduce your portfolio's overall volatility. For example, when stock markets are down, bonds or real estate may provide more stability.

2. Sector Diversification:

Within each asset class, it's important to diversify

across sectors. In a stock portfolio, this could mean investing in technology, healthcare, finance, consumer goods, and other industries. Different sectors often perform well at different times, and sector diversification reduces the risk of one industry's downturn severely impacting your portfolio.

3. Geographic Diversification:

Expanding your investments to include international markets can help mitigate the risks associated with any one country's economic performance. Domestic investments may be affected by political, economic, or regulatory issues, while investments in global markets can provide opportunities for growth in regions with strong economic prospects.

4. Investment Style Diversification:

You can also diversify by incorporating different investment styles into your portfolio. For instance, growth investments focus on companies expected to grow faster than the market, while value investments target undervalued companies with solid fundamentals. A balanced mix of growth, value, and income-producing investments can help manage risk in various market environments.

5. Time Diversification (Dollar-Cost Averaging):

Dollar-cost averaging is a strategy where you invest a fixed amount of money at regular intervals, regardless of market conditions. This approach helps reduce the risk of investing a large sum at an inopportune time, such as when markets are at a peak. Over time, dollar-cost averaging helps smooth out the effects of market volatility, as you buy more shares when prices are low and fewer shares when prices are high.

6. Alternative Investments:

Alternative investments, such as commodities, hedge funds, private equity, or infrastructure, often have low correlations with traditional stocks and bonds. Including a small allocation of these alternative assets can provide additional diversification benefits, further reducing overall portfolio risk.

By incorporating these diversification strategies, you can create a well-balanced portfolio that reduces risk while offering the potential for growth across different asset classes and market conditions.

Balancing Risk and Reward

Investing successfully requires balancing the risks you take with the rewards you expect to earn. This balance is influenced by your investment horizon, financial goals, and risk tolerance.

Key Concepts for Balancing Risk and Reward

1. Risk-Return Trade-off:

The risk-return trade-off is the principle that higher potential returns are generally associated with higher risk. For example, stocks typically offer higher long-term returns than bonds, but they are also more volatile. Understanding your personal risk tolerance helps you determine the appropriate balance of risk and reward for your portfolio.

2. Expected Return:

The expected return is the projected profit or growth from an investment, based on its past performance and future outlook. While no return is guaranteed, understanding the expected return of an investment allows you to assess whether it is worth the associated risk.

3. Risk-Adjusted Return:

Risk-adjusted return is a measure that compares an investment's return relative to the risk it carries. A common way to assess risk-adjusted return is through the Sharpe ratio, which shows how much return an investment has provided per unit of risk. The higher the Sharpe ratio, the better an investment's risk-adjusted return.

4. Investment Horizon:

Your investment horizon—how long you plan to hold an investment—plays a critical role in determining your risk tolerance. If you have a long investment horizon, you can afford to take more risks, as you have time to recover from short-term losses. Shorter investment horizons, such as for retirement or college savings, may require more conservative, lower-risk investments to preserve capital.

5. Diversification:

Once again, diversification is essential in balancing risk and reward. By investing in a variety of assets that behave differently under different conditions, you reduce the chance of significant losses while still pursuing potential gains. A diversified portfolio provides more stable, consistent returns over the long term.

By understanding these concepts, you can better align your investment strategy with your financial goals and risk tolerance, ensuring that you take the right amount of risk for the rewards you seek.

Tools for Managing Investment Risk

There are several tools and techniques you can use to manage risk in your investment portfolio. These tools help protect your investments from significant losses and ensure that your portfolio remains aligned with your financial goals.

Key Risk Management Tools

1. Diversification:
As discussed, diversification is one of the simplest and most effective risk management tools. Spreading your investments across different asset classes and sectors helps reduce the overall volatility of your portfolio.

2. Asset Allocation:
Asset allocation is the process of dividing your portfolio among different asset classes, such as stocks, bonds, and cash, based on your risk tolerance and financial goals. Regularly reviewing and rebalancing your asset allocation ensures that your portfolio remains aligned with your objectives, even as market conditions change.

3. Stop-Loss Orders:
A stop-loss order is a tool that automatically sells a security when it reaches a predetermined price. This can help limit your losses by exiting a position before it declines further. Stop-loss orders are particularly useful in volatile markets or for riskier investments.

4. Hedging:

Hedging involves using financial instruments, such as options or futures, to protect your portfolio from potential losses. For example, you could purchase put options on a stock you own, which allows you to sell the stock at a set price if the market declines. While hedging can be complex, it's an effective way to reduce risk in specific situations.

5. Rebalancing:

Rebalancing is the practice of adjusting your portfolio's asset allocation back to its original target after market fluctuations have caused it to drift. For example, if your stock holdings have increased in value relative to your bond holdings, rebalancing involves selling some of the stocks and buying more bonds to maintain your desired allocation. This ensures that your portfolio's risk level remains consistent with your goals.

6. Insurance:

Certain types of insurance, such as life, health, or property insurance, can help protect your wealth and reduce financial risk. Life insurance can provide financial support to your family in the event of your death, while health insurance protects you from the high cost of medical bills. Property insurance safeguards your assets in case of damage or loss.

Real-Life Case Studies in Risk Management

Looking at real-life examples can help illustrate how effective risk management strategies work in practice. Here are a few notable case studies:

1. The 2008 Financial Crisis:

During the global financial crisis of 2008, many investors who were heavily invested in real estate or financial stocks experienced severe losses. However, those who had diversified portfolios, including safer assets like bonds or international investments, were better able to weather the downturn. This highlights the importance of diversification and maintaining a balanced asset allocation.

2. The Dot-Com Bubble:

The dot-com bubble of the late 1990s saw a dramatic rise in technology stocks, followed by a steep crash in 2000. Many investors lost significant wealth as overvalued tech companies collapsed. Investors who had diversified their portfolios across other sectors and asset classes experienced less severe losses and were able to recover more quickly.

3. Warren Buffett's Risk Management Strategy:

Warren Buffett, one of the world's most successful investors, is known for his disciplined approach to risk management. Buffett focuses on investing in high-quality companies with strong fundamentals and holding them for the long term. He avoids speculative investments and emphasizes the importance of understanding the risks associated with any investment. His long-term approach and attention to risk management have helped him achieve consistent success.

4. A Small Business Owner's Diversified Portfolio:

A small business owner who invested a portion of their profits in a diversified portfolio of stocks, bonds, and real estate was able to protect their wealth during market downturns. By rebalancing their portfolio regularly and using stop-loss orders, they mitigated risks while achieving steady growth over time. This case study underscores the importance of maintaining a disciplined, diversified approach to investing.

Conclusion: Effective Risk Management for Long-Term Success

Risk management is an essential component of successful investing. By understanding the different types of risks, diversifying your portfolio, balancing risk and reward, and using tools like stop-loss orders, rebalancing, and insurance, you can protect your investments and achieve long-term financial growth. Learning from real-life case studies and incorporating these strategies into your investment plan will help you build a resilient portfolio that can withstand market volatility while meeting your financial goals.

CHAPTER 8: THE IMPACT OF INFLATION

Inflation is one of the most important economic factors that can significantly affect both personal finances and investments. Its ability to erode the purchasing power of money and affect the overall economy makes it crucial for investors to understand how inflation works and how to protect themselves against its effects. In this chapter, we will explore the definition and causes of inflation, its effects on purchasing power and investments, strategies to hedge against inflation, and how historical data and future projections can help guide investment decisions.

Definition and Effects of Inflation

What Is Inflation?

Inflation refers to the rate at which the general level of

prices for goods and services rises over time, reducing the purchasing power of money. When inflation occurs, each unit of currency buys fewer goods and services, which means that the value of money diminishes as time passes. It's a common economic phenomenon, and managing its impact is essential for long-term financial planning.

Inflation is typically measured using indices like the Consumer Price Index (CPI) or the Producer Price Index (PPI):
- The CPI tracks the average price changes over time for a basket of goods and services that households commonly purchase, such as food, transportation, and healthcare.
- The PPI measures price changes from the perspective of producers, which can eventually pass through to consumer prices.

Causes of Inflation

There are several underlying causes of inflation, each affecting the economy in different ways:

1. Demand-Pull Inflation:
   This type of inflation occurs when the demand for goods and services exceeds supply. As demand rises, businesses increase prices because consumers are willing to pay more. For instance, during periods of economic growth or when governments inject money into the economy, increased consumer spending can drive inflation higher.

2. Cost-Push Inflation:
   Cost-push inflation arises when the cost of production increases, leading businesses to raise prices to maintain profit margins. This can occur due to rising wages, higher

raw material costs, or supply chain disruptions.

3. Built-In Inflation:

Sometimes referred to as wage-price inflation, this occurs when people expect prices to rise, and therefore, they demand higher wages. Businesses, in turn, raise prices to offset the higher labour costs, leading to a self-sustaining inflation cycle.

Effects on Purchasing Power

One of the most direct effects of inflation is its erosion of purchasing power. When prices increase, the same amount of money buys fewer goods and services than before. For example, if inflation is 3% annually, a product that costs $100 this year will cost $103 next year, meaning you will need more money to maintain the same standard of living.

For savers and investors, inflation can pose a significant challenge. If your savings or investments are not growing at a rate that outpaces inflation, your real purchasing power is declining. This makes it essential to invest in assets that can provide returns above the inflation rate to maintain or increase your wealth over time.

Impact on Investments

Inflation affects different types of investments in various ways, and understanding these effects is critical for maintaining a healthy portfolio. Some key impacts include:

1. Fixed-Income Investments (Bonds):

Inflation is particularly harmful to bonds and other fixed-income securities. As inflation rises, the real value of the interest payments from bonds decreases. This is because the fixed interest rate doesn't change, but the purchasing power of the payments declines. Inflation-protected securities, like Treasury Inflation-Protected Securities (TIPS), are designed to counteract this effect by adjusting with inflation.

2. Stocks:
Stocks have historically served as a hedge against inflation. Companies can pass on rising production costs to consumers through higher prices, maintaining their profit margins. However, not all stocks are equally affected. Companies with strong pricing power, such as those in essential goods or sectors with inelastic demand (like utilities), may perform better during inflationary periods.

3. Real Estate:
Real estate often benefits from inflation because property values and rental income tend to rise with increasing prices. Additionally, real estate offers a tangible asset that typically holds or increases in value over time, providing an effective hedge against inflation.

4. Commodities:
Commodities such as gold, silver, and oil have historically performed well during periods of high inflation. As the prices of goods and services rise, so do the values of these tangible assets. Investors often turn to commodities to preserve purchasing power during inflationary times.

5. Cash:
Holding large amounts of cash during inflation is generally unwise, as the purchasing power of cash

decreases over time. Inflation erodes the value of money held in savings or checking accounts that do not generate returns higher than the inflation rate.

6. Inflation-Protected Securities:

Investments like TIPS provide a safeguard against inflation by adjusting the principal value based on changes in the Consumer Price Index (CPI). These securities are designed specifically to protect investors from the negative effects of rising prices.

How Inflation Impacts Investments

Let's take a closer look at how inflation affects different types of investments and what steps investors can take to mitigate these impacts.

Bonds and Fixed-Income Investments

Inflation has a particularly strong effect on bonds and other fixed-income investments because they provide predetermined interest payments. When inflation rises, these fixed payments lose purchasing power. For example, if a bond pays 3% interest and inflation rises to 5%, the real return on the bond becomes negative, meaning the investor is effectively losing money in terms of purchasing power.

However, investors can counteract this risk by diversifying into inflation-protected securities like TIPS. These bonds adjust their principal value based on inflation, ensuring that the real value of the investment is preserved even as prices rise.

Stocks

Stocks have historically performed well during inflationary periods, but not all stocks are created equal. Companies with strong pricing power—those that can pass on higher costs to consumers without losing business—tend to perform best. Sectors like consumer staples, healthcare, and utilities often have more stability during inflationary periods because their products and services remain in demand regardless of price increases.

Growth stocks, which rely on future earnings, may suffer during inflation as the value of their future cash flows is discounted more heavily. On the other hand, dividend-paying stocks provide a steady income stream that can help offset inflation's effects, particularly if the companies regularly increase their dividends.

Real Estate

Real estate investments tend to benefit from inflation because property values and rental incomes typically rise as the cost of living increases. Real estate investment trusts (REITs), which allow investors to gain exposure to real estate without directly owning property, are a popular way to hedge against inflation. As inflation pushes up property prices and rents, REITs often see increased income and asset value growth.

Commodities

Commodities, such as gold, oil, and agricultural products, are often seen as a safe haven during inflation. When inflation rises, the value of these tangible assets typically increases. Gold, in particular, has been used as a store of value for centuries and often performs well during inflationary periods because it is considered a hedge against currency devaluation.

Strategies to Hedge Against Inflation

Protecting your investments from inflation is crucial for maintaining your purchasing power and long-term financial health. Here are some effective strategies to hedge against inflation:

1. Invest in Stocks

Stocks, especially those in inflation-resistant sectors like consumer staples, healthcare, and utilities, provide a good hedge against inflation. These companies often have the ability to raise prices to offset rising costs, thus maintaining their profit margins. Additionally, dividend-paying stocks can offer a steady income that grows over time, helping to combat inflation.

2. Real Estate Investments

Real estate is a traditional hedge against inflation because property values and rental income tend to rise as inflation increases. Investing in residential or commercial properties can provide both income and long-term appreciation. For investors who prefer not to own physical property, REITs offer a more liquid option that still provides exposure to real estate's inflation-hedging benefits.

3. Commodities and Precious Metals

Commodities like gold, silver, and oil typically perform well during inflationary periods. As the cost of goods and services rises, the value of these tangible assets tends to increase. Adding a small allocation of commodities to your portfolio can help protect against inflation, particularly in times of economic uncertainty.

4. Treasury Inflation-Protected Securities (TIPS)

For investors looking for a direct hedge against inflation, TIPS are a reliable option. These securities adjust their principal value based on changes in the CPI, meaning your investment is automatically protected from inflation. While the yield on TIPS may be lower than traditional bonds, they offer a safeguard in periods of rising inflation.

5. Global Diversification

Investing in international assets can help hedge against domestic inflation. Economies around the world may experience inflation at different rates, and by diversifying globally, you reduce the risk of being overly exposed to inflation in any one country. International stocks and bonds offer additional diversification and can help balance the impact of inflation in your home country.

6. Short-Term Bonds

Short-term bonds are less sensitive to inflation and interest rate changes compared to long-term bonds. Investing in short-term bonds can help reduce the impact of rising inflation and interest rates on your fixed-income portfolio. Because these bonds mature quickly, they can be reinvested at higher rates if inflation continues to rise.

7. Dividend-Paying Stocks

Dividend-paying stocks can provide a reliable income stream that can outpace inflation, especially if the companies have a history of increasing their dividends over time. Sectors such as utilities, consumer goods, and healthcare often include companies that pay steady dividends, offering some protection during inflationary periods.

Historical Data and Inflation

Looking at historical data can provide valuable insights into how different asset classes have performed during periods of high inflation. This information can help investors understand how to position their portfolios to withstand inflation's impact.

Stocks and Inflation

Stocks have generally provided positive real returns during periods of moderate inflation. However, during times of extreme inflation, such as the 1970s, stock performance became more volatile. Companies with strong pricing power or those in industries less affected by rising costs tend to perform better during inflationary periods.

Bonds and Inflation

Bonds, particularly long-term bonds, have historically underperformed during high inflation because their fixed interest payments lose purchasing power. Short-term bonds, on the other hand, tend to perform better as they are less sensitive to rising interest rates and inflation.

Real Estate and Inflation

Real estate has traditionally been one of the best performers during periods of high inflation. Rising property values and rental income help offset the effects of inflation. Commercial real estate and rental properties often see an increase in demand during inflationary periods, further driving up prices and income potential.

Commodities and Inflation

Commodities such as gold and oil have consistently performed well during periods of high inflation. As inflation pushes up the cost of goods and services, the value of tangible assets like commodities tends to rise. This makes commodities a popular choice for investors looking to hedge against inflation.

Future Projections and Planning

Planning for the future involves considering potential inflation scenarios and adjusting your investment strategy accordingly. By staying informed about economic conditions and inflation forecasts, you can better prepare for how inflation may affect your financial goals.

Economic Outlook

Monitoring inflation trends and the broader economic outlook is essential for planning. Central bank policies, fiscal stimulus, and global economic conditions all influence inflation levels. For example, expansionary monetary policies or increased government spending can fuel inflation, while tighter fiscal policies may help contain it.

Investment Strategy Adjustments

Your investment strategy should account for inflation risks. Consider diversifying your portfolio to include assets that typically perform well during inflationary periods, such as stocks, real estate, and commodities. Regularly review your asset allocation to ensure it remains aligned with your financial goals and the current economic environment.

Emergency Fund

Maintaining an emergency fund is essential for financial security, particularly during inflationary times. Having enough cash set aside for emergencies ensures that you won't need to sell investments at an inopportune time, such as during a market downturn. While inflation can erode the value of cash, an emergency fund provides a critical safety net for unforeseen expenses.

Long-Term Perspective

A long-term perspective is essential when investing. While inflation can erode short-term returns, a well-diversified portfolio that includes inflation-resistant assets can help you achieve your financial goals over the long term. Focusing on long-term growth, rather than reacting to short-term inflationary pressures, is key to successful investing.

Conclusion: Protecting Against Inflation for Financial Success

Inflation is an inevitable part of the economic landscape, but understanding its impact and taking proactive steps can help you protect your investments and preserve your wealth. By diversifying your portfolio, investing in inflation-resistant assets, and maintaining a long-term perspective, you can mitigate the effects of inflation and ensure that your financial goals remain on track. Regularly reviewing and adjusting your investment strategy based on inflation trends will help you stay prepared for whatever the future holds.

CHAPTER 9: TAX IMPLICATIONS

Maximizing Returns By Navigating Taxation On Investments

Tax implications are an integral part of managing your investments and achieving long-term financial success. Every investment decision has a tax consequence, whether it's buying and selling stocks, receiving dividends, or contributing to tax-advantaged accounts. A sound understanding of the various tax rules that apply to different types of investments can help you enhance your after-tax returns and ensure that your financial goals are met in the most tax-efficient way possible.

In this chapter, we will explore the key types of taxes that apply to investments, strategies for tax-efficient investing, the benefits of tax-advantaged accounts, and real-life examples that show how proper tax planning can significantly boost your investment results.

Understanding Tax on Investments

Investing wisely is not just about picking the right assets; it's also about understanding the tax implications that come with them. Various types of taxes apply to different investment activities, and managing these effectively can enhance your overall returns. Let's look at some of the main types of taxes on investments.

1. Capital Gains Tax

Capital gains tax is levied on the profit made from selling an asset, such as stocks, bonds, or real estate. The tax rate depends on how long you hold the investment before selling it.

- Short-Term Capital Gains: These apply to assets held for one year or less. Gains from short-term investments are taxed at your ordinary income tax rate, which can be significantly higher than long-term capital gains rates.

- Long-Term Capital Gains: If you hold an asset for more than one year, the profit qualifies as long-term capital gains, which are taxed at a lower rate. Depending on your income level, the tax rate on long-term gains could be 0%, 15%, or 20%, making it a more favourable option for long-term investors.

2. Dividends

Dividends are payments made by companies to their shareholders, typically from profits. Dividends can be classified as either qualified or non-qualified, and they are taxed differently:

- Qualified Dividends: These are taxed at the lower long-term capital gains tax rate, making them more tax-efficient for investors who hold dividend-paying stocks for longer periods.

- Non-Qualified Dividends: These dividends are taxed at the higher ordinary income tax rate. Non-qualified dividends usually come from real estate investment trusts (REITs) or other assets that do not meet the criteria for qualified dividends.

3. Interest Income

Interest income from investments such as bonds, savings accounts, or certificates of deposit (CDs) is generally taxed as ordinary income. Unlike dividends or capital gains, which may benefit from lower tax rates, interest income does not enjoy any tax advantages. Therefore, tax-efficient strategies become especially important for investors heavily invested in fixed-income securities.

4. Tax-Advantaged Accounts

Tax-advantaged accounts such as 401(k)s, IRAs, and Roth IRAs offer significant benefits for reducing your tax burden. Contributions to these accounts can grow tax-deferred or tax-free, depending on the type of account, providing an opportunity to maximize your investment returns over time.

5. Tax Loss Harvesting

Tax loss harvesting is a strategy used to offset capital gains by selling investments that have declined in value. The losses from these sales can reduce your taxable gains, and, in some cases, can be used to offset up to

$3,000 of ordinary income per year. Any unused losses can be carried forward to future years, making tax loss harvesting a valuable tool for reducing your overall tax liability.

Understanding these tax implications allows you to make more informed decisions about when and how to invest, ensuring that your investment returns are maximized after accounting for taxes.

Strategies for Tax Efficiency

One of the most powerful ways to maximize your investment returns is by being strategic about the taxes you pay. By utilizing tax-efficient strategies, you can minimize your tax liability and keep more of your hard-earned money. Below are some strategies that can help you manage the tax burden on your investments:

1. Utilize Tax-Advantaged Accounts

Contributing to tax-advantaged accounts such as 401(k)s, IRAs, and Roth IRAs is one of the best ways to grow your investments while minimizing taxes. These accounts offer different types of tax benefits:

- Traditional 401(k) or IRA: Contributions are made with pre-tax dollars, reducing your taxable income for the year. The funds grow tax-deferred, meaning you won't pay taxes on the investment gains until you withdraw the money in retirement.

- Roth IRA: Contributions are made with after-tax dollars, but withdrawals in retirement are tax-free. This can be a powerful tool for long-term tax planning, especially if you expect to be in a higher tax bracket when you retire.

2. Hold Investments for the Long Term

Holding investments for more than one year can significantly reduce your tax liability due to the lower long-term capital gains tax rate. By focusing on long-term growth rather than frequent trading, you not only save on taxes but also reduce transaction costs, which can further erode returns.

3. Tax Loss Harvesting

Tax loss harvesting allows you to sell losing investments to offset the gains from winning investments. This strategy can lower your overall taxable income and improve your after-tax returns. Be aware of the wash sale rule, which prevents you from repurchasing the same or a substantially identical security within 30 days of the sale.

4. Invest in Tax-Efficient Funds

Some mutual funds and exchange-traded funds (ETFs) are designed with tax efficiency in mind. These tax-efficient funds minimize capital gains distributions, which can help reduce your tax liability. Index funds, in particular, tend to be more tax-efficient because they have lower turnover compared to actively managed funds.

5. Asset Location

Asset location is a strategy where you place different types of investments in the most tax-advantageous accounts. For example, it's generally more tax-efficient to place tax-inefficient assets like bonds in tax-deferred accounts (e.g., traditional IRAs or 401(k)s) and tax-efficient assets like index funds in taxable accounts.

By doing so, you can minimize the taxes on your investments while maximizing growth.

6. Reinvest Dividends

Reinvesting dividends can help you take advantage of compounding returns. If you hold dividend-paying stocks in a tax-advantaged account, you won't need to worry about paying taxes on the dividends right away, allowing you to grow your investments more efficiently.

By implementing these tax-efficient strategies, you can significantly reduce the amount of taxes you pay and keep more of your investment returns, which helps you reach your financial goals faster.

Tax-Advantaged Accounts

Tax-advantaged accounts offer powerful opportunities to grow your wealth while minimizing taxes. Let's explore some of the most common types of tax-advantaged accounts and how they work.

1. 401(k) Plans

401(k) plans are employer-sponsored retirement accounts that allow employees to make contributions with pre-tax dollars. This reduces your taxable income in the year of the contribution, and the funds grow tax-deferred until you withdraw them in retirement, at which point they are taxed as ordinary income.

Many employers also offer matching contributions, which can further boost your retirement savings. It's wise to contribute at least enough to get the full employer match, as this is essentially "free money" for your retirement.

2. Traditional IRAs

A traditional Individual Retirement Account (IRA) allows you to contribute pre-tax dollars, similar to a 401(k), but the contribution limits are lower. The funds grow tax-deferred, and withdrawals in retirement are taxed as ordinary income. Traditional IRAs are a good option if you want to reduce your taxable income now while saving for retirement.

3. Roth IRAs

A Roth IRA allows you to contribute after-tax dollars, but the benefit comes later, as the investment grows tax-free, and withdrawals in retirement are also tax-free. Roth IRAs are particularly beneficial if you expect to be in a higher tax bracket in the future, as you'll pay taxes at today's lower rates and avoid them in retirement.

4. Health Savings Accounts (HSAs)

Health Savings Accounts (HSAs) are tax-advantaged accounts designed to help individuals save for medical expenses. Contributions to an HSA are tax-deductible, the funds grow tax-free, and withdrawals for qualified medical expenses are also tax-free. HSAs are an excellent tool for long-term savings, as any unused funds can continue to grow year after year, and they can be used for medical expenses in retirement.

5. 529 Plans

A 529 plan is a tax-advantaged savings plan designed to help families save for education expenses. Contributions to a 529 plan grow tax-free, and withdrawals used for qualified education expenses, such as tuition, books, and fees, are also tax-free. These accounts are a great way to save for a child's or grandchild's future education while enjoying significant tax benefits.

6. Coverdell Education Savings Accounts (ESAs)

Like 529 plans, Coverdell ESAs offer tax-free growth and withdrawals for qualified education expenses. However, they have lower contribution limits and additional income restrictions. Coverdell ESAs are another option for parents and guardians who want to save for their children's education with tax-free growth.

Real-Life Examples and Case Studies

To better understand the impact of tax strategies on investments, let's look at a few real-life examples and case studies that illustrate how tax planning can make a big difference in your financial outcomes.

1. Maximizing Retirement Savings

John contributes the maximum allowable amount to his 401(k) each year. By doing so, he not only reduces his taxable income but also benefits from the tax-deferred growth of his investments. Over the years, John's contributions and investment gains compound without being taxed, allowing him to build a substantial retirement nest egg. When John retires, he will pay taxes on his withdrawals, but his overall savings will be much higher due to the tax-deferred growth.

2. Roth IRA Conversion

Sarah has been contributing to a traditional IRA for

several years. However, in a year when her income is lower, she decides to convert her traditional IRA to a Roth IRA. By paying taxes on the conversion now, Sarah secures tax-free growth and tax-free withdrawals in retirement. This strategy reduces her overall tax liability, as she will not have to pay taxes on the future growth of her investments.

3. Tax Loss Harvesting

David experiences a downturn in his stock portfolio and decides to sell some underperforming stocks at a loss. He uses the losses to offset gains from other investments, reducing his overall taxable income. David then reinvests the proceeds from the sale into different securities, allowing him to maintain his investment strategy while benefiting from lower taxes.

4. Education Savings

Lisa starts contributing to a 529 plan for her child's future education. The contributions grow tax-free over time, and when her child is ready for college, Lisa can withdraw the funds tax-free for qualified education expenses. This provides significant tax savings and helps Lisa fund her child's education without taking on debt.

These examples demonstrate how tax-efficient strategies can enhance investment returns and help achieve financial goals. By adopting similar approaches, you can maximize your after-tax returns and secure long-term financial success.

Working with Tax Professionals

Given the complexity of tax laws and regulations, working with a tax professional can be invaluable in optimizing your investment strategy. Here's how a tax professional can assist you:

1. Tax Planning

A tax professional can help you develop a comprehensive tax plan that aligns with your financial goals. By identifying opportunities for tax savings, they can recommend strategies to minimize your tax liability while maximizing your investment returns.

2. Tax Preparation

Tax professionals are well-versed in the intricacies of tax laws and can prepare and file your tax returns accurately. They will ensure that you take advantage of all available deductions, credits, and other tax benefits.

3. Investment Advice

Tax professionals can offer guidance on the tax implications of different investment options. Whether you're deciding between a traditional IRA and a Roth IRA or looking for ways to minimize capital gains taxes, a tax advisor can help you make informed decisions that improve your after-tax returns.

4. Estate Planning

For those looking to pass on wealth to the next generation, tax professionals can assist with estate planning. They can help minimize estate taxes and ensure that your assets are transferred smoothly to your heirs through strategies like trusts, gifting, and charitable donations.

5. Retirement Planning

Tax professionals can help you navigate the complexities of retirement planning, including managing required minimum distributions (RMDs) and minimizing taxes on retirement income. They can recommend strategies to ensure that your retirement savings are optimized for tax efficiency.

6. Audit Support

In the event that you are audited by the IRS, having a tax professional on your side is crucial. They can provide support, represent you in dealings with the IRS, and help resolve any issues that arise during the audit.

Conclusion: Navigating Taxes for Long-Term Financial Success

Understanding and managing the tax implications of your investments is essential for maximizing your after-tax returns and achieving your financial goals. By employing tax-efficient strategies, utilizing tax-advantaged accounts, and working with knowledgeable tax professionals, you can significantly reduce your tax burden and keep more of your investment gains. Tax planning should be an ongoing part of your investment strategy, helping you navigate the complexities of tax laws while ensuring your long-term financial success.

CHAPTER 10: BUILDING A COMPOUND INTEREST PLAN

Building a successful compound interest plan is the cornerstone of achieving long-term financial success. Whether you are saving for retirement, a home, or simply building wealth, a structured plan that harnesses the power of compound interest can help you reach your goals. This chapter provides a detailed guide on how to develop and manage a compound interest plan, from setting financial goals to monitoring progress and adjusting as needed.

Setting Financial Goals

The foundation of any financial plan begins with setting clear, measurable goals. Without a target, it's difficult to build a plan or track progress. Setting financial goals allows you to stay focused and motivated, ensuring that every step you take brings you closer to your desired outcome.

Steps to Setting Effective Financial Goals

1. Identify Your Financial Goals:

The first step is to clearly define what you want to achieve with your investments. Your goals might range from saving for retirement, buying a house, paying off debt, funding your children's education, or creating an emergency fund. Each of these goals will require different strategies, timelines, and levels of risk tolerance.

2. Make Goals Specific and Measurable:

Vague goals are hard to achieve. Instead of saying, "I want to save for retirement," make the goal specific and measurable: "I want to save $1 million by age 65 for my retirement." This gives you a clear target to work toward, making it easier to track your progress.

3. Set Realistic Time Frames:

Establish a realistic time frame for each of your goals. Short-term goals may focus on immediate needs like building an emergency fund, while long-term goals might include retirement planning, which could span decades. Having a time frame helps you determine how aggressively you need to save and what type of investments are best suited for each goal.

4. Assess Your Risk Tolerance:

Your ability and willingness to take risks is an important factor in choosing your investment strategy. Risk tolerance depends on your financial situation, age, goals, and comfort level with market volatility. A younger investor saving for retirement might have a higher tolerance for risk, allowing for more aggressive investments, while someone nearing retirement may prefer safer, more conservative options.

5. Create a Detailed Plan:
Once you've identified your goals and time frames, the next step is to create a plan to achieve them. This plan should outline your savings strategy, the types of investments you'll pursue, and how often you will review and adjust your plan. Setting a monthly or annual savings target is critical for staying on track.

By setting specific, measurable, and realistic financial goals, you lay the foundation for a well-structured compound interest plan that aligns with your financial aspirations.

Creating a Step-by-Step Plan

After setting your financial goals, you need to create a detailed action plan that will guide your saving and investing efforts. This plan breaks down the steps required to reach your goals and outlines how to apply the power of compound interest to grow your wealth over time.

Steps to Develop Your Plan

1. Calculate Your Savings Rate:
To reach your financial goals, you must first determine how much you need to save each month. Use an online compound interest calculator to estimate the required savings rate based on your target amount, expected

annual return, and the time frame. This gives you a clear idea of how much you need to invest regularly to achieve your desired outcome.

2. Choose Appropriate Investment Options:

Once you know how much you need to save, the next step is selecting the right investment vehicles. Your choices will depend on your risk tolerance and financial goals. A diversified portfolio of stocks, bonds, real estate, and other assets can help balance risk and reward, providing both growth potential and stability. Consider low-cost index funds, exchange-traded funds (ETFs), or mutual funds for long-term growth.

3. Set Up Automatic Contributions:

One of the easiest ways to stay consistent with your savings plan is by setting up automatic contributions to your investment accounts. This ensures that you save regularly without having to think about it. Automating your savings reduces the temptation to spend the money elsewhere and keeps you on track to reach your goals.

4. Monitor and Adjust Your Plan:

Regularly reviewing your progress is essential for staying on course. Check your investment portfolio periodically to see if you're on track to meet your goals. If your portfolio becomes unbalanced due to market fluctuations, consider rebalancing to maintain your desired asset allocation. Adjust your strategy based on market conditions but avoid reacting too quickly to short-term volatility.

5. Stay Informed and Adapt:

Staying informed about economic trends, tax law changes, and investment opportunities can help you make better decisions. Regularly educating yourself on these topics allows you to adjust your investment strategy as needed. Keep in mind that your financial situation and goals may change over time, so be prepared to adapt your plan when necessary.

Following these steps creates a clear, actionable path toward achieving your financial goals with the power of compound interest.

Tools and Resources for Managing Your Plan

Managing a compound interest plan can seem complex, but there are many tools and resources available to help simplify the process. Leveraging these resources can save you time, increase efficiency, and provide you with valuable insights to enhance your financial decision-making.

Key Tools and Resources

1. Compound Interest Calculators:
These online tools help you calculate the growth of your investments over time, factoring in interest rates, time frames, and contributions. They allow you to estimate how much your investments will grow and adjust your savings rate accordingly. Popular calculators can be found on financial websites like Bankrate or Investor.gov.

2. Financial Planning Software:
Comprehensive financial planning platforms, such as Personal Capital, Mint, or Quicken, provide a holistic view of your finances. These tools track your income, expenses, investments, and savings, helping you set

and monitor goals. Some also offer budgeting tools, retirement planning features, and personalized advice.

3. Investment Platforms:

Online brokerage accounts like Vanguard, Fidelity, and Charles Schwab offer a wide range of investment options and tools for managing your portfolio. These platforms provide educational resources, market insights, and tools to help you track your investments and make informed decisions.

4. Robo-Advisors:

For those who prefer a hands-off approach, robo-advisors such as Betterment and Wealthfront provide automated investment management. Based on your financial goals and risk tolerance, robo-advisors create a diversified portfolio and automatically adjust it over time to keep you on track.

5. Financial Advisors:

If you need more personalized guidance, working with a financial advisor can provide valuable support. Advisors can help you develop a tailored plan, select appropriate investments, and offer ongoing advice to keep you on track. They are particularly useful for more complex financial situations or those nearing retirement.

By utilizing these tools and resources, you can simplify the process of managing your compound interest plan and stay organized as you work toward your financial goals.

Monitoring Progress

One of the most important aspects of a successful

compound interest plan is regularly monitoring your progress. This allows you to see how your investments are performing, adjust your strategy when necessary, and stay motivated as you work toward your financial goals.

How to Effectively Monitor Your Plan

1. Set Regular Review Dates:

Schedule specific times to review your financial plan. Whether quarterly, biannually, or annually, these review sessions should involve assessing your progress toward your goals and determining if any adjustments are necessary. Regular reviews keep you accountable and provide an opportunity to celebrate small victories along the way.

2. Track Investment Performance:

Use financial software or your brokerage platform to monitor the performance of your investments. Compare your actual returns to your expected returns to ensure you are on track. If your returns are not meeting expectations, investigate whether external market factors or internal issues, such as unbalanced asset allocation, are to blame.

3. Rebalance Your Portfolio:

Over time, market movements can cause your portfolio to drift away from your desired asset allocation. For example, if stocks perform particularly well, your portfolio may become more heavily weighted toward equities, increasing your overall risk. Rebalancing involves selling some of the overperforming assets and buying underperforming ones to restore your original allocation.

4. Review and Adjust Goals:

As your financial situation changes, you may need to revisit and adjust your goals. Perhaps you received a raise, had a child, or bought a home. Life events often require recalibration of your goals and savings strategies. Regularly reassessing your goals ensures that they remain relevant and achievable.

5. Stay Updated on Economic and Market Trends:

Staying informed about economic conditions, interest rate changes, and tax law revisions can help you make strategic adjustments to your plan. While it's important not to overreact to short-term market volatility, keeping an eye on long-term trends can provide insight into how to adjust your portfolio for optimal performance.

Monitoring your progress ensures that you remain on track to meet your financial objectives and allows for any necessary course corrections along the way.

Adjusting the Plan as Needed

No financial plan is set in stone. Life is full of changes, and your compound interest plan needs to be flexible enough to adapt to those changes. Whether due to shifting personal circumstances, market conditions, or evolving financial goals, it's important to revisit and adjust your plan periodically.

How to Adjust Your Plan Effectively

1. Assess Life Changes:

Significant life events, such as getting married, having children, changing jobs, or experiencing a health crisis, may require you to adjust your financial goals and strategy. For instance, a new job may come with a higher salary, enabling you to increase your savings rate and accelerate progress toward your goals.

2. Revisit and Reprioritize Goals:

As your financial situation evolves, some goals may become more

urgent, while others may take a backseat. Reevaluate your goals to determine which ones still align with your priorities. For example, if you've achieved one goal early, such as paying off debt, you may want to redirect your efforts toward a different goal, like saving for a child's education or increasing retirement contributions.

3. Adjust Savings Rates:

If you receive a raise, inheritance, or other financial windfall, consider increasing your monthly contributions to your investment accounts. By doing so, you can reach your goals faster or accumulate more wealth over the same time frame. Conversely, if you encounter financial difficulties, you may need to temporarily reduce your savings rate until your situation stabilizes.

4. Modify Asset Allocation:

As you get closer to achieving your goals, particularly long-term ones like retirement, you may need to shift your portfolio to a more conservative allocation. For instance, someone nearing retirement might reduce exposure to stocks and increase holdings in bonds or other lower-risk assets to preserve capital.

5. Seek Professional Advice:

If you encounter significant changes or uncertainties in your financial life, consider seeking the guidance of a financial advisor. An advisor can help you make informed decisions about adjusting your plan, navigating complex financial situations, and maintaining your focus on long-term success.

Adjusting your compound interest plan when necessary ensures that your strategy remains aligned with your current financial situation and goals. Flexibility is key to ensuring that unexpected events or changes don't derail your progress.

Conclusion: The Power of Planning and Compound Interest

Building a compound interest plan is a powerful way to achieve long-term financial success. By setting clear goals, creating a detailed plan, and leveraging tools and resources, you can maximize the benefits of compounding to grow your wealth. Monitoring your progress regularly and adjusting your plan as needed ensures that you stay on track, even when life throws unexpected changes your way.

The power of compound interest lies in its ability to turn small, consistent contributions into significant financial growth over time. The earlier you start, the greater the impact, making it essential to act now, no matter your financial goals. By following the steps outlined in this chapter, you can harness the potential of compound interest and build a strong foundation for your financial future.

CHAPTER 11: BEHAVIOURAL FINANCE

Mastering The Psychological Side Of Investing

When it comes to investing, making sound financial decisions is not just about understanding markets or knowing which stocks to pick. It's also about understanding the human mind. Behavioural finance explores the psychological factors that influence investment decisions, helping investors recognize and manage the emotional biases that can derail even the most well-planned strategies.

In this chapter, we will delve into how cognitive biases, emotional responses, and herd behaviour impact financial decisions. We will explore tools and strategies for overcoming these challenges, develop a long-term investment mindset, and examine case studies that highlight how behavioural finance affects real-world investments.

Psychological Factors in Investing

While traditional finance theory assumes investors are rational decision-makers, behavioural finance acknowledges that psychological factors often lead to irrational behaviours. Recognizing these mental and emotional influences is crucial to avoiding mistakes and making better investment choices.

1. Cognitive Biases

Cognitive biases are mental shortcuts or tendencies that cause people to make errors in judgment. When it comes to investing, these biases can lead to poor decision-making. Here are a few of the most common biases:

- Overconfidence Bias: Many investors overestimate their knowledge or abilities, leading them to take on excessive risks. Overconfidence can cause people to trade too frequently, believe they can time the market, or assume they have more control over outcomes than they actually do.

- Anchoring Bias: This bias occurs when investors rely too heavily on a specific piece of information—such as the price they paid for a stock—when making decisions. Anchoring can prevent investors from recognizing when an asset is over- or undervalued based on current market conditions.

- Confirmation Bias: Investors tend to seek out

information that confirms their pre-existing beliefs and ignore data that contradicts them. This can lead to a narrow perspective and failure to consider alternative views or adjust to new realities.

By being aware of these biases, you can take steps to avoid irrational decisions and improve the objectivity of your investment process.

2. Emotional Responses

Emotions play a major role in investing. Market volatility, headlines, and personal circumstances can trigger strong emotional reactions, which can cloud judgment. Two of the most powerful emotions in investing are fear and greed.

- Fear: Fear often leads investors to panic during market downturns, selling off assets at a loss. This is particularly common during stock market crashes when people worry about losing everything. Selling based on fear can lock in losses and prevent recovery when markets eventually rebound.

- Greed: On the flip side, greed can cause investors to take on excessive risk, particularly when chasing high returns. This is often seen during market bubbles, where investors rush to buy into rapidly rising assets without fully understanding the risks. Greed can also lead to a lack of diversification, as investors concentrate too much money in one "hot" sector or asset.

Managing emotional responses is key to maintaining a level-headed approach to investing, especially during volatile periods.

3. Behavioural Finance

Behavioural finance is the study of how psychological factors influence financial decisions. It recognizes that while people strive to make rational decisions, they are often swayed by emotional and cognitive biases. Understanding the principles of behavioural finance can help you identify when these factors are influencing your own decisions and take steps to mitigate their impact.

For example, prospect theory suggests that investors feel the pain of losses more intensely than the pleasure of gains—a concept known as loss aversion. This can lead to holding onto losing investments for too long or being too conservative to avoid risk, even when taking on some risk is necessary for long-term growth.

4. Herd Behaviour

Herd behaviour occurs when investors follow the actions of the larger group, regardless of their own research or beliefs. When everyone else is buying a particular stock or asset, it's tempting to jump on the bandwagon out of fear of missing out (FOMO). However, this can lead to market bubbles or investing in overvalued assets that may crash when the hype fades.

While it's natural to want to follow others, it's important to conduct independent research and make decisions based on sound analysis rather than popular trends.

5. Loss Aversion

Loss aversion is a psychological concept where people are more motivated to avoid losses than they are to achieve gains. For example, losing $100 feels more painful than the pleasure of gaining $100, even though the financial impact is the same. This fear of losses can cause investors to make poor decisions, such as holding onto losing stocks longer than necessary in hopes that they will rebound or avoiding risk altogether.

Understanding loss aversion can help you make more balanced and objective decisions. It's important to recognize that losses are a normal part of investing, and by focusing on long-term goals, you can minimize the emotional impact of short-term setbacks.

Overcoming Emotional Biases

Emotional biases are one of the biggest challenges investors face. Learning to manage emotions and maintain discipline is essential for long-term success. Here are strategies to help you overcome emotional biases and make better investment decisions.

1. Develop a Clear Investment Plan

One of the best ways to manage emotional reactions is to create a detailed investment plan that outlines your goals, risk tolerance, and strategy. When you have a plan in place, it's easier to stick to it during periods of market volatility, preventing panic-driven decisions.

Your plan should include:
- Financial goals: What are you saving for, and what is your time horizon?
- Risk tolerance: How much risk are you comfortable with, and how do you plan to balance risk and return?
- Investment strategy: How will you allocate your investments across different asset classes? How often will

you review and rebalance your portfolio?

2. Stick to Your Plan

It's easy to get swept up in the excitement of a rising market or the fear of a falling one. However, sticking to your plan is critical. During market downturns, it's tempting to sell investments and "cut losses." Conversely, during market booms, you may feel pressured to invest heavily in hot assets. Both of these scenarios can lead to costly mistakes. Sticking to your long-term plan helps you avoid impulsive decisions driven by emotions.

3. Diversify Your Portfolio

Diversification is a powerful tool for managing risk and minimizing emotional reactions. By spreading your investments across a range of asset classes—stocks, bonds, real estate, and commodities—you reduce the impact of market fluctuations on your portfolio. This makes it easier to remain calm during market downturns because your entire portfolio is less likely to experience significant losses at once.

4. Automate Your Investments

One of the best ways to avoid emotional decisions is to automate your investments. By setting up regular, automated contributions to your investment accounts, you can stay disciplined in your savings strategy. Automated investing allows you to take advantage of dollar-cost averaging, where you invest the same amount of money at regular intervals regardless of market conditions, smoothing out the impact of market volatility.

5. Practice Patience

Successful investing requires patience. The most significant returns often come from holding investments over the long term and allowing compound interest to work its magic. Reacting to short-term market fluctuations can undermine long-term growth. By keeping your focus on long-term goals and staying patient, you can ride out market volatility and benefit from the eventual recovery.

6. Seek Professional Advice

A financial advisor can provide objective guidance and help you stay focused on your goals. During volatile periods, an advisor can offer a steadying influence, helping you avoid emotionally driven decisions. Advisors can also help you adjust your portfolio to reflect changes in your financial situation or risk tolerance.

Developing a Long-term Mindset

One of the most important traits of successful investors is the ability to maintain a long-term perspective. By focusing on long-term goals and staying committed to your investment strategy, you can overcome the emotional temptations of short-term market movements.

1. Focus on Your Financial Goals

Your financial goals are the foundation of your investment strategy. Whether you're saving for retirement, buying a house, or building an emergency fund, keeping your long-term goals in mind helps you stay motivated and prevents short-term distractions from derailing your plan.

2. Understand Market Cycles

Markets go through cycles of growth, decline, and recovery. Understanding that these cycles are normal can help you remain calm during downturns. Instead of reacting emotionally to falling markets, remind yourself that recovery is a natural part of the cycle. Long-term investors who hold on through market downturns often benefit from the eventual rebound.

3. Ignore Short-term Noise

Financial news can be overwhelming, and headlines are often designed to provoke emotional responses. While it's important to stay informed, try not to react to every piece of market news. Instead, focus on the fundamentals of your investments and their long-term potential.

4. Reinvest Dividends

Reinvesting dividends is a simple yet powerful way to compound your returns over time. When you receive dividends, instead of spending them or withdrawing them, reinvest them into your portfolio. This practice helps accelerate your portfolio's growth and brings you closer to achieving your financial goals.

5. Stay Informed and Educated

A solid understanding of investing principles can help you maintain a long-term perspective. By educating yourself about investment strategies, market trends, and financial concepts, you'll feel more confident in your decisions and less likely to make emotional, short-term moves.

6. Regularly Review Your Portfolio

While maintaining a long-term mindset is crucial, it's still important to periodically review your portfolio. Life circumstances change, and you may need to adjust your investment strategy as you get closer to your goals. Reviewing your portfolio once or twice a year allows you to adjust as needed without reacting to short-term market movements.

Case Studies on Behavioural Finance

Understanding how psychological factors affect real-life investment decisions can provide valuable insights. Here are several case studies that highlight the impact of behavioural finance in action.

1. The Dot-Com Bubble

During the late 1990s, the stock market experienced a massive boom in technology stocks, driven by excitement over the potential of the internet. Many investors ignored traditional metrics like earnings and valuation, believing that technology stocks would continue to rise indefinitely. This herd behaviour, combined with overconfidence, fuelled the dot-com bubble.

When the bubble burst in 2000, many investors who had followed the crowd experienced significant losses. Those who had remained disciplined, focusing on fundamentals and maintaining diversified portfolios, fared much better during the downturn.

2. The 2008 Financial Crisis

The 2008 financial crisis was a period of extreme market volatility and fear. As stock prices plummeted, many investors panicked and sold their investments at significant losses. However, those who maintained a long-term perspective and resisted the urge to sell were able to recover as the market eventually rebounded. The crisis underscored the importance of avoiding emotionally driven decisions and sticking to a long-term strategy.

3. Bitcoin Mania

In 2017, Bitcoin and other cryptocurrencies experienced a meteoric rise in value, driven by speculative frenzy and FOMO (fear of missing out). Many investors jumped into the market without fully understanding the risks, chasing high returns based on hype rather than solid fundamentals. When the market corrected, prices of cryptocurrencies fell sharply, leading to substantial losses for those who had bought in at the peak.

4. Warren Buffett's Long-term Success

Warren Buffett, one of the most successful investors in history, is known for his disciplined, long-term approach to investing. Buffett avoids short-term speculation, instead focusing on buying high-quality companies at reasonable prices and holding them for the long haul. His success demonstrates the value of patience, discipline, and sticking to fundamental investment principles.

Tools and Techniques for Managing Behavioural Biases

While understanding behavioural biases is important, it's equally critical to have tools and techniques to manage them. Here are several resources and strategies that can help you stay disciplined and make rational decisions.

1. Investment Apps

Investment apps like Betterment and Wealthfront offer automated investment management based on your financial goals and risk tolerance. These platforms help you stay disciplined by automating contributions, portfolio rebalancing, and tax-loss harvesting, reducing the emotional influence on your decisions.

2. Financial Planning Software

Using financial planning software like Personal Capital or Mint can give you a comprehensive view of your financial situation. These tools help you track your investments, set financial goals, and monitor your progress, making it easier to stay focused on the big picture and avoid reacting to short-term market fluctuations.

3. Educational Resources

Books, online courses, and financial blogs are excellent resources for deepening your understanding of behavioural finance and investing. By regularly educating yourself, you become more equipped to make informed decisions and less likely to fall prey to biases or emotional reactions.

4. Mindfulness Techniques

Practicing mindfulness, such as meditation and deep breathing, can help you manage stress and maintain emotional balance, especially during periods of market volatility. By staying calm and centred, you can make more rational decisions.

5. Regular Reviews

Set regular intervals to review your investment plan and portfolio. This allows you to make any necessary adjustments while staying committed to your long-term goals. Periodic reviews can also help you reinforce a long-term mindset and avoid emotionally driven decisions.

6. Professional Advice

Working with a financial advisor can provide valuable guidance, helping you navigate the psychological challenges of investing. Advisors offer objective advice, helping you avoid common behavioural traps and stay focused on your financial goals.

Conclusion: Harnessing Behavioural Finance for Investment Success

Behavioural finance teaches us that our emotions and cognitive biases can greatly impact our investment decisions. By understanding these psychological factors and implementing strategies to overcome them, you can become a more disciplined and effective investor.

Whether it's creating a detailed investment plan, automating your investments, or seeking professional advice, the key to long-term success lies in managing emotions, sticking to a well-thought-out strategy, and keeping a clear focus on your financial goals. The more you understand the role of psychology in finance, the better equipped you'll be to navigate the ups and downs of the market and achieve lasting financial success.

CHAPTER 12: THE ROLE OF FINANCIAL ADVISORS

Managing personal finances can be a complex and challenging endeavour. Whether you're planning for retirement, managing investments, or navigating taxes and estate planning, professional guidance can make a significant difference. Financial advisors play a crucial role in helping individuals achieve their financial goals by offering expert advice, personalized strategies, and ongoing support.

This chapter will explore the importance of working with financial advisors, how to choose the right one, the benefits of professional advice, and strategies for building a strong working relationship with your advisor. Through case studies and practical tips, you'll understand the value that financial advisors bring to your financial journey.

Finding the Right Advisor

Choosing the right financial advisor is one of the most important steps in securing your financial future. The right advisor will understand your unique needs, provide tailored solutions, and offer support throughout your financial journey. Here's a step-by-step guide to finding the perfect fit.

Steps to Finding the Right Financial Advisor:

1. Identify Your Needs:

Before you start searching for an advisor, take time to identify what type of help you need. Are you looking for investment management, retirement planning, tax planning, or estate planning? Knowing your specific needs will help you find an advisor with expertise in the relevant areas.

2. Research Credentials:

It's important to choose a financial advisor with the right credentials. Look for certifications such as:

- Certified Financial Planner (CFP): This certification indicates that the advisor has met rigorous education, experience, and ethical standards.

- Chartered Financial Analyst (CFA): A CFA designation shows expertise in investment management and financial analysis.

- Certified Public Accountant (CPA): A CPA can provide valuable advice on tax planning and accounting issues.

3. Check Experience:

An advisor's experience matters, especially when dealing with complex financial issues. Look for someone who has experience in the specific areas that align with your goals. Ask about their track record, how long they've been in the industry, and their experience with clients similar to you.

4. Evaluate Services:

Different advisors offer different services. Some may specialize in investment management, while others offer comprehensive financial planning, including retirement, tax, and estate planning. Make sure the advisor provides the full range of services that match your needs.

5. Understand Fees:

Financial advisors have various fee structures. Some charge a percentage of assets under management (AUM), others charge hourly rates, and some work on a flat-fee basis. It's essential to understand how your advisor charges for their services and ensure that it aligns with your budget and financial goals.

6. Interview Multiple Advisors:

Don't rush into choosing an advisor. Interview several candidates to find the best fit for your needs. Ask about their approach to financial planning, investment philosophy, and how they handle client relationships. A good rapport and trust are essential for a long-term working relationship.

By carefully considering these factors, you can find an advisor who is not only qualified but also a good fit for your personal financial needs.

Benefits of Professional Advice

Working with a financial advisor offers numerous advantages that can help you achieve your financial goals more effectively. Advisors bring a wealth of knowledge, an objective perspective, and the ability to manage complex financial matters that might be challenging to navigate on your own.

Key Benefits of Professional Financial Advice:

1. Expertise:

Financial advisors have extensive training and knowledge in various areas of personal finance, such as investments, retirement planning, and taxes. Their expertise allows them to provide informed recommendations and strategies tailored to your unique financial situation.

2. Personalized Guidance:

An advisor works with you to develop a financial plan that is customized to your goals, risk tolerance, and life circumstances. Whether you're saving for retirement, buying a home, or planning your estate, a financial advisor can create a strategy that aligns with your specific needs.

3. Objective Perspective:

Emotions like fear or greed can cloud your judgment when making financial decisions. A financial advisor provides an objective viewpoint, helping you stay focused on your long-term goals rather than reacting impulsively to market fluctuations or short-term news.

4. Comprehensive Planning:

Financial advisors take a holistic approach to your financial situation. They consider your income, savings, investments, insurance, taxes, and estate planning to develop a well-rounded strategy that covers all aspects of your financial life.

5. Time Savings:

Managing your finances, especially as they grow more complex, can be time-consuming. A financial advisor handles the heavy lifting—monitoring investments, researching options, and adjusting—so you can focus on other priorities while staying confident that your financial future is in good hands.

6. Accountability:

One of the often-overlooked benefits of working with an advisor is accountability. Advisors help keep you on track, reminding you of your goals and providing regular reviews and updates to ensure your financial plan remains aligned with your life's changes.

By leveraging the expertise and personalized approach of a financial advisor, you can more effectively achieve your financial objectives while avoiding common pitfalls and mistakes.

Working with Advisors

Once you've found the right financial advisor, building a strong working relationship is crucial for achieving your financial goals. A successful advisor-client relationship is built on trust, communication, and collaboration. Here are tips for getting the most out of your relationship with your financial advisor.

Tips for Working Effectively with Your Advisor:

1. Communicate Your Goals Clearly:
The first step in a successful partnership with your advisor is to communicate your financial goals clearly. Whether your objectives involve saving for your children's education, retiring early, or building an investment portfolio, your advisor needs to understand your priorities to create a plan that suits you.

2. Be Transparent About Your Financial Situation:
To create an accurate and effective financial plan, your advisor needs complete and honest information about your financial situation. Be transparent about your income, debts, savings, assets, and expenses. Withholding information can lead to flawed financial advice.

3. Ask Questions:
Don't hesitate to ask questions if something isn't clear. Whether it's about your investment strategy, how fees work, or specific financial products, a good advisor will take the time to explain things in a way that you can understand. Asking questions helps you stay informed and confident in your financial decisions.

4. Schedule Regular Reviews:
Financial plans are not static. Your goals, circumstances, and market conditions can change over time, so regular reviews are essential. Schedule periodic meetings with your advisor to assess your progress, make any necessary adjustments, and ensure your strategy is still aligned with your objectives.

5. Provide Feedback:

Open communication is essential for a healthy advisor-client relationship. If you're unsatisfied with any aspect of the service or feel your needs aren't being met, provide constructive feedback. Advisors appreciate input, as it helps them tailor their services to better suit your needs.

6. Stay Informed:

While your advisor is there to guide you, it's still important to stay involved and informed about your financial plan. Being an active participant in your financial journey ensures that you understand the decisions being made and can offer input when necessary.

By maintaining open communication and being actively involved in your financial plan, you can build a strong partnership with your advisor, leading to better financial outcomes.

Questions to Ask Advisors

Asking the right questions can help you make an informed decision when choosing a financial advisor. These questions will provide insight into their qualifications, approach, and the value they can bring to your financial journey.

Essential Questions to Ask When Choosing a Financial Advisor:

1. What are your credentials?

Understanding your advisor's qualifications is critical. Ask about their certifications, education, and experience.

Look for designations like CFP (Certified Financial Planner) or CFA (Chartered Financial Analyst), which indicate a high level of professional expertise.

2. What services do you offer?

Advisors offer different types of services. Make sure the advisor can provide the specific help you need, whether that's investment management, tax planning, estate planning, or comprehensive financial planning.

3. How do you get paid?

Ask about the advisor's fee structure and make sure it's transparent. Some advisors charge a percentage of the assets they manage, while others work on an hourly basis or charge a flat fee. Make sure you're comfortable with the fee arrangement and understand how it aligns with your financial goals.

4. What is your investment philosophy?

Every advisor has a different approach to investing. Some may focus on passive, long-term strategies, while others take a more active, hands-on approach. Make sure their investment philosophy aligns with your goals, risk tolerance, and investment timeline.

5. How will you develop my financial plan?

Ask about the process the advisor will follow to create your financial plan. Understanding how they gather information, assess your needs, and develop recommendations will give your insight into how personalized and comprehensive their service is.

6. How often will we meet or communicate?

Regular communication is essential for staying on track with your financial goals. Find out how often you'll have meetings, whether in person or virtual, and how frequently they will update you on your portfolio's performance.

7. Can you provide references?

A reputable advisor should be willing to provide references from past or current clients. Speaking with these individuals can give you a better sense of the advisor's approach, reliability, and success in helping others achieve their financial goals.

By asking these questions, you'll be able to evaluate potential advisors effectively and select one who aligns with your needs and preferences.

Case Studies

Real-life examples can illustrate the tangible benefits of working with a financial advisor. Here are a few case studies that show how professional guidance can help individuals meet their financial objectives.

1. Retirement Planning Success: Jane's

Story

Jane was in her early 50s and realized she had not saved enough for retirement. She sought the help of a financial advisor, who helped her create a plan to maximize her 401(k) contributions and invest in tax-efficient accounts like a Roth IRA. The advisor also assisted Jane in selecting investments that aligned with her risk tolerance and long-term goals.

By working closely with her advisor and following a disciplined savings and investment strategy, Jane was able to build a comfortable retirement fund. Today, she enjoys her retirement with the peace of mind that her financial future is secure.

2. Investment Management for Long-term Growth: Tom's Experience

Tom, a 40-year-old professional, wanted to grow his wealth but didn't have the expertise or time to manage his investments. He hired a financial advisor who developed a diversified investment portfolio tailored to Tom's risk tolerance and financial goals.

Over the years, Tom's advisor regularly reviewed the portfolio, adjusting based on market conditions and Tom's evolving financial situation. As a result, Tom achieved consistent returns, allowing him to grow his wealth significantly over time.

3. Tax Planning and Optimization: Sarah's Strategy

Sarah was a high-income earner and was concerned about the impact of taxes on her investments. She consulted with a financial advisor, who helped her develop a tax-efficient investment strategy. This included maximizing contributions to tax-advantaged accounts like Roth IRAs and HSAs and implementing tax-loss harvesting to offset capital gains.

The result was a significant reduction in Sarah's tax liability, allowing her to keep more of her investment gains and grow her wealth more efficiently.

4. Estate Planning with Financial Guidance: John and Mary's Plan

John and Mary, a couple in their 60s, wanted to ensure

their estate would be passed on to their children with minimal taxes and legal hurdles. They worked with a financial advisor who helped them create a comprehensive estate plan. This included drafting a will, setting up trusts for their children, and planning charitable donations.

The estate plan ensured that John and Mary's assets were distributed according to their wishes while minimizing estate taxes, giving them peace of mind about their legacy.

Conclusion: The Value of Financial Advisors

Financial advisors provide invaluable guidance, expertise, and support, helping individuals navigate the complexities of personal finance. Whether you're planning for retirement, managing investments, optimizing taxes, or preparing an estate plan, a qualified advisor can help you achieve your financial goals with confidence and clarity.

By finding the right advisor, working collaboratively, and staying actively involved in your financial journey, you can build a solid foundation for long-term financial success. The insights and strategies offered by a financial advisor not only save you time and effort but also enhance your ability to make informed, objective decisions that benefit your financial future.

CHAPTER 13: TECHNOLOGY AND INVESTING

In recent years, technology has revolutionized the world of investing, making it more accessible, efficient, and personalized than ever before. From online trading platforms to robo-advisors, mobile apps, and advanced data analytics, technology has dramatically changed how we manage our money and make investment decisions. In this chapter, we'll explore how technology has impacted investing, the tools and apps available, the rise of automated investment services, and how investors can use technology to conduct research and plan for the future.

The Impact of Technology on Investing

Technology has democratized investing, allowing more people to participate in financial markets and manage their own portfolios. In the past, investing was often seen as a domain reserved for professionals or the wealthy. Today, anyone with a smartphone can invest in stocks, bonds, or even cryptocurrencies with just a few taps. Here are the keyways technology has transformed the investing landscape:

1. Online Trading Platforms

Online trading platforms have made buying and selling securities easier, faster, and cheaper. In the past, investors had to rely on brokers to execute trades, often paying high fees. Now, platforms like Robinhood, ETRADE, and Fidelity allow investors to trade stocks, bonds, ETFs, and options from the comfort of their homes, often at little or no cost. These platforms offer easy access to global financial markets and provide a range of tools for tracking performance, researching investments, and making informed decisions.

2. Robo-Advisors

Robo-advisors are automated platforms that manage investments using algorithms. These services have gained popularity for their low fees and hands-off approach, making investing accessible to a broader audience. Robo-advisors like Betterment and Wealthfront analyze your financial goals, risk tolerance, and time horizon to create a diversified portfolio of investments. They handle everything from asset allocation to rebalancing and tax optimization, making investing simple for those who may not have the time or expertise to manage their own portfolios.

3. Mobile Apps

With the rise of mobile apps, managing investments

has never been more convenient. Apps like Acorns, Robinhood, and Stash allow you to monitor your portfolio, execute trades, and access financial news from your smartphone. Whether you're a seasoned investor or just getting started, these apps provide tools that make investing more accessible, often with intuitive interfaces and features that simplify the process.

4. Big Data and Analytics

Data has always been at the heart of investing, but advances in big data and analytics have taken research and decision-making to new heights. Investors now have access to real-time market data, detailed financial reports, and sophisticated analytics tools that can help identify patterns and predict market movements. Tools like Bloomberg, Morningstar, and Yahoo Finance provide comprehensive market data and insights, helping investors make more informed decisions.

5. Blockchain and Cryptocurrencies

Blockchain technology has introduced new asset classes, such as cryptocurrencies like Bitcoin and Ethereum, and has the potential to revolutionize financial transactions by providing greater transparency and security. For investors, this opens up new opportunities to diversify their portfolios with digital assets. While still in its infancy, blockchain's decentralized nature promises to disrupt traditional banking and investing, with far-reaching implications for the future of finance.

6. Social Trading

Social trading platforms allow investors to follow and replicate the trades of successful investors. Platforms like eToro have made it possible for beginners to learn from experienced traders by copying their strategies. Social trading democratizes access to investment strategies and fosters a collaborative environment, where investors can share insights and ideas.

The ongoing evolution of technology continues to open up new opportunities for investors, making the process more efficient and transparent. Understanding these technological advancements can help investors take advantage of the tools available to enhance their investment strategy.

Investment Apps and Tools

Investment apps have become a central part of modern investing, offering convenience, ease of use, and powerful features that help investors manage their portfolios and make better financial decisions. Whether you're new to investing or an experienced trader, there are apps and tools designed to meet your needs. Here are some of the most popular options:

1. Robinhood

Robinhood offers commission-free trading for stocks, ETFs, options, and cryptocurrencies, making it a popular choice for both new and seasoned investors. Its clean, easy-to-use interface has revolutionized the way people trade by eliminating fees, allowing users to start investing with small amounts of money.

2. Acorns

Acorns takes the concept of micro-investing to the

next level by automatically investing your spare change. Every time you make a purchase, Acorns rounds up the transaction to the nearest dollar and invests the difference in a diversified portfolio. This app is ideal for beginners looking to get started with small investments over time.

3. Stash

Stash combines education with investing, offering personalized investment recommendations and guidance to help users build diversified portfolios. The app allows users to invest in fractional shares, meaning you can invest in big-name stocks and ETFs with as little as $5. Stash also emphasizes financial literacy, offering articles and videos to help users learn more about investing.

4. Betterment

As one of the leading robo-advisors, Betterment provides automated investment management with features like goal-based investing, tax-loss harvesting, and retirement planning tools. Betterment tailors portfolios to your financial goals, automatically rebalancing your investments to keep them aligned with your risk tolerance and objectives.

5. Wealthfront

Wealthfront offers similar automated investment services, along with financial planning tools that help you save for retirement, education, and other financial goals. Wealthfront also provides tax-efficient investing strategies and offers a cash management account with a competitive interest rate.

6. Personal Capital

Personal Capital provides a more comprehensive suite of financial tools, including investment tracking, retirement planning, and budgeting. It allows users to see all their financial accounts in one place, offering a holistic view of their financial situation. Personal Capital also provides personalized investment advice and a dedicated financial advisor for those who want more hands-on support.

By using these apps and tools, investors can stay organized, track their portfolios, and make more informed decisions. The accessibility of these platforms has empowered millions of people to take control of their financial futures.

Automated Investment Services

Automated investment services, commonly known as robo-advisors, have grown rapidly in popularity due to their ability to provide low-cost, efficient investment management. For those who want professional portfolio management without the high fees or complexity, robo-advisors offer a compelling solution.

How Automated Investment Services Work:

1. Algorithm-Based Management:
Robo-advisors use algorithms to create and manage investment portfolios. After assessing your financial goals, risk tolerance, and time horizon, the algorithm builds a diversified portfolio designed to meet your objectives. The process is fully automated, meaning

there's no need for human intervention.

2. Low Fees:

One of the biggest advantages of robo-advisors is their low cost. Traditional financial advisors often charge 1% or more of assets under management, while robo-advisors typically charge between 0.25% and 0.50%. This makes them an attractive option for investors looking to keep costs low.

3. Diversification:

Robo-advisors automatically create diversified portfolios by investing in a mix of asset classes, including stocks, bonds, and real estate. This reduces risk and helps smooth out returns over time.

4. Rebalancing:

One of the most important aspects of maintaining a balanced portfolio is rebalancing, which involves adjusting your investments to maintain your desired asset allocation. Robo-advisors handle rebalancing automatically, ensuring that your portfolio stays in line with your goals.

5. Tax Efficiency:

Many robo-advisors offer tax-efficient investing strategies, such as tax-loss harvesting, which involves selling losing investments to offset gains, thereby reducing your tax liability.

6. Accessibility:

Robo-advisors have made investing more accessible to a broader audience, especially for those with smaller account balances. Many platforms have low minimum investment requirements and provide easy-to-use interfaces that simplify the process of managing money.

Overall, automated investment services provide a hands-off approach to investing, allowing users to benefit from professional management without the need for constant monitoring or decision-making.

Using Technology for Research

Technology has made it easier than ever to conduct thorough investment research, giving individual investors access to the same information and tools that professionals use. Here are some ways you can leverage technology to make informed investment decisions:

1. Financial News and Analysis

Staying informed about market trends, economic developments, and company news is critical for making timely investment decisions. Platforms like Bloomberg, Reuters, and CNBC provide real-time financial news and analysis, helping investors stay up to date on the latest market movements.

2. Market Data Platforms

Tools like Yahoo Finance, Google Finance, and Morningstar offer comprehensive financial data, including stock prices, financial statements, historical performance, and analyst ratings. These platforms are invaluable for analyzing potential investments and monitoring portfolio performance.

3. Investment Screeners

Investment screeners allow you to filter stocks, ETFs, and mutual funds based on specific criteria, such as market capitalization, dividend yield, and price-to-earnings ratio. Tools like Finviz and Zacks offer customizable screeners that can help you identify investment opportunities that match your strategy.

4. Social Media

Social media platforms like Twitter and LinkedIn have become powerful tools for investors. By following financial influencers, analysts, and news outlets, you can gain valuable insights and stay connected to the financial community. Engaging with other investors can help you learn from their experiences and discover

new opportunities.

5. Research Reports

Many investment firms, such as Fidelity, Vanguard, and Charles Schwab, provide in-depth research reports on stocks, bonds, and other assets. These reports offer professional analysis and recommendations that can help you make more informed investment decisions.

6. Online Courses and Webinars

Whether you're a beginner or looking to deepen your knowledge, online courses and webinars are excellent resources for learning about investing. Platforms like Coursera, Udemy, and Khan Academy offer a wide range of courses covering topics from the basics of investing to advanced financial strategies.

By using these tools, you can conduct detailed investment

research and stay informed about the markets, helping you make better financial decisions.

Future Trends in Technology and Investing

As technology continues to evolve, new trends are emerging that will further shape the future of investing. Here are some of the key trends to watch:

1. Artificial Intelligence (AI) and Machine Learning

AI and machine learning are expected to play a significant role in the future of investment management. These technologies can analyze vast amounts of data to identify patterns and make predictions, enhancing investment strategies and decision-making. AI-driven platforms may offer even more personalized investment advice, tailored to an individual's unique financial situation.

2. Blockchain and Cryptocurrencies

Blockchain technology and cryptocurrencies like Bitcoin and Ethereum have the potential to revolutionize financial transactions and create new investment opportunities. As the regulatory framework around these assets matures, more investors may incorporate digital currencies into their portfolios. Blockchain technology itself could improve transparency and security in financial markets, offering new ways to execute trades and manage assets.

3. Robo-Advisors 2.0

The next generation of robo-advisors will likely integrate more advanced AI and machine learning, offering enhanced personalization and predictive financial planning. These platforms may be able to anticipate your financial needs, adjusting your investment strategy based on real-time data and changes in your life circumstances.

4. Sustainable Investing

Environmental, social, and governance (ESG) factors are becoming increasingly important to investors who want to align their portfolios with their values. In the future, technology will play a larger role in helping investors assess ESG risks and opportunities, making sustainable investing more accessible and measurable.

5. Fintech Integration

The integration of financial technology (fintech) into traditional financial services is expected to expand, making investing more efficient and accessible. From mobile banking to digital wallets and peer-to-peer lending platforms, fintech innovations will continue to disrupt traditional financial models, offering more convenience and flexibility to investors.

6. Personalization Through Data Analytics

Advances in data analytics will enable more personalized investment experiences. Investors can expect customized portfolios, tailored financial advice, and real-time adjustments based on their individual preferences, financial goals, and market conditions.

By staying informed about these future trends, investors can leverage new technologies to enhance their investment strategies and achieve their financial goals.

Conclusion: Embracing Technology in Your Investment Strategy

Technology has changed the way we invest, providing tools and platforms that make investing more accessible, efficient, and personalized. Whether you're using robo-advisors for automated portfolio management, investment apps to track your portfolio, or conducting research using advanced analytics, embracing technology can help you make better financial decisions.

As new trends like artificial intelligence, blockchain, and fintech integration continue to shape the investment landscape, staying informed and adapting to these changes will be key to success. By leveraging the latest technological advancements, you can enhance your investment strategy, optimize your returns, and take control of your financial future.

CHAPTER 14: RETIREMENT PLANNING

Retirement planning is one of the most critical aspects of financial management, as it ensures that you can maintain financial security and live comfortably after your working years. Proper retirement planning allows you to build a solid financial foundation, manage risks, and enjoy your retirement years without worrying about money. This chapter explores the importance of retirement planning, strategies for investments, the power of compound interest, different retirement account options, and essential tax considerations.

The Importance of Retirement Planning

Retirement planning is more than just saving money; it involves preparing for a future where you can live comfortably without the need for employment income.

Here's why planning for retirement is crucial:

1. Financial Independence

One of the primary goals of retirement planning is to achieve financial independence, where you no longer need to work to maintain your lifestyle. With a proper plan, you can build a financial cushion that allows you to live on your savings and investments during your retirement years. This means you won't have to rely on family members, social security, or government assistance.

2. Longevity

People are living longer, thanks to advances in healthcare and overall well-being. A longer lifespan means you might spend several decades in retirement. Without a plan, you risk running out of money later in life, which could result in financial struggles. Proper retirement planning ensures that your funds last as long as you do, providing peace of mind.

3. Inflation

Inflation is a critical factor to consider when planning for retirement. Over time, inflation erodes the purchasing power of your money. What costs $100 today may cost much more in 20 or 30 years. Without careful planning, your retirement savings may not keep up with rising prices, leaving you with less purchasing power. A solid plan will include investments that can outpace inflation, preserving your financial stability.

4. Healthcare Costs

As you age, healthcare expenses tend to increase. Whether it's medical treatment, prescriptions, or long-term care, healthcare can become a significant cost during retirement. Planning ahead can ensure you have sufficient funds and insurance coverage to meet these expenses without compromising your lifestyle.

5. Tax Efficiency

Retirement planning also involves choosing the right tax-advantaged accounts and strategies to minimize your tax liability. Making use of tax-deferred or tax-free accounts helps you grow your savings while minimizing the amount of tax you pay on withdrawals during retirement.

6. Legacy and Estate Planning

Beyond your personal needs, retirement planning allows you to plan for the legacy you want to leave behind. This includes estate planning, which ensures that your assets are distributed according to your wishes, minimizing estate taxes, and reducing the administrative burden for your heirs.

Proper retirement planning enables you to enjoy financial security, maintain your standard of living, and achieve peace of mind throughout your golden years.

Strategies for Retirement Investments

Building a robust investment portfolio is essential for ensuring that you have enough money to live comfortably during retirement. A well-constructed strategy can help grow and preserve your wealth, manage risks, and support your financial goals.

1. Diversify Your Portfolio

Diversification is one of the most fundamental principles of investing, and it's especially important for retirement planning. By spreading your investments across different asset classes—such as stocks, bonds, real estate, and cash—you reduce the impact of poor performance in any one area. Diversification helps balance risk and return, ensuring that your portfolio can weather market volatility and still grow over time.

2. Asset Allocation

As you approach retirement, your investment strategy should evolve to reflect your changing goals and risk tolerance. Younger investors with many years before retirement can afford to take on more risk, with a higher allocation in growth-oriented assets like stocks. As you near retirement, it's generally wise to shift toward more conservative investments like bonds and cash, which focus on preserving capital rather than achieving high returns.

3. Consistent Contributions

Regular contributions to your retirement accounts can have a significant impact over time. Whether through an employer-sponsored plan like a 401(k) or an Individual Retirement Account (IRA), contributing consistently helps your savings grow, thanks to the power of compounding. Automated contributions ensure that you save regularly, even if you don't always have time to monitor your investments.

4. Tax-Advantaged Accounts

Take full advantage of tax-advantaged accounts, such as 401(k)s, Traditional IRAs, and Roth IRAs. These accounts offer valuable tax benefits that can enhance your retirement savings. Contributions to 401(k)s and Traditional IRAs are tax-deferred, meaning you don't pay taxes on the money you contribute until you withdraw it in retirement. Roth IRAs, on the other hand, provide tax-free withdrawals in retirement, as contributions are made with after-tax dollars.

5. Periodic Rebalancing
Over time, some investments in your portfolio may grow faster than others, causing your asset allocation to drift from its target. Rebalancing involves selling assets that have performed well and buying those that have underperformed, ensuring that your portfolio stays aligned with your goals and risk tolerance. This disciplined approach prevents your portfolio from becoming too risky or too conservative as you near retirement.

6. Planning for Healthcare Costs
It's essential to plan for healthcare expenses in retirement, as these can become a significant part of your budget. One option is to contribute to a Health Savings Account (HSA), which offers tax benefits and allows you to save for medical expenses. HSAs are especially valuable because contributions, growth, and withdrawals for qualified medical expenses are all tax-free.

By implementing these strategies, you can build a strong retirement portfolio that supports your financial goals and provides security during your retirement years.

Using Compound Interest for Retirement

Compound interest is one of the most powerful tools for growing your retirement savings. It allows your investments to grow exponentially over time by earning returns on both your initial investment and the interest that has already accumulated. Here's how you can maximize the power of compound interest in your retirement planning:

1. Start Early

The earlier you start saving for retirement, the more time you give compound interest to work its magic. Even small contributions made early in your career can grow into significant sums by the time you retire. Starting early gives your investments more time to compound, making it easier to reach your financial goals with less effort.

2. Consistent Contributions

Making regular contributions to your retirement accounts is crucial for taking full advantage of compound interest. Whether it's monthly, quarterly, or annually, consistently adding to your retirement savings ensures that your investments continue to grow over time. Automated contributions can help you stay disciplined and maintain consistency.

3. Reinvesting Dividends

Dividends are a form of income paid by some stocks and mutual funds. Reinvesting these dividends—rather than taking them as cash—allows them to generate even more earnings. Over time, reinvesting dividends can significantly boost your retirement savings, as they contribute to the compounding effect.

4. Increase Contributions Over Time

As your income grows, it's a good idea to increase your retirement contributions. Consider setting aside a portion of any raises, bonuses, or windfalls for your retirement accounts. Increasing your contributions can accelerate your savings and help you take greater advantage of compound interest.

5. Maximize Employer Matching Contributions

Many employers offer matching contributions to 401(k) plans, which is essentially free money. If your employer offers a match, contribute enough to take full advantage of it. For example, if your employer matches 50% of your contributions up to a certain limit, you should contribute at least enough to receive the full match. This extra boost can significantly increase your retirement savings over time.

6. Stay Invested

It's important to maintain a long-term perspective when investing for retirement. Market fluctuations are inevitable, but staying invested allows your money to continue compounding over time. Avoid making impulsive decisions based on short-term market volatility and focus on the long-term growth of your investments.

By leveraging the power of compound interest, you can grow your retirement savings more efficiently and achieve financial security for your future.

Retirement Account Options

There are several types of retirement accounts available, each with unique benefits and considerations. Choosing the right accounts for your situation can help you maximize your savings and reduce your tax liability. Here are some common retirement account options:

1. 401(k) Plans

A 401(k) is an employer-sponsored retirement plan that

allows you to contribute pre-tax dollars, reducing your taxable income in the year you contribute. The money grows tax-deferred, meaning you won't pay taxes on your earnings until you withdraw the funds in retirement. Many employers also offer matching contributions, which can significantly boost your savings.

2. Traditional IRAs

A Traditional IRA is an individual retirement account that allows for tax-deferred growth. Contributions may be tax-deductible, reducing your taxable income in the year you contribute. Like a 401(k), you won't pay taxes on your earnings until you make withdrawals in retirement.

3. Roth IRAs

A Roth IRA differs from a Traditional IRA in that contributions are made with after-tax dollars, but qualified withdrawals in retirement are tax-free. This makes Roth IRAs a valuable option for those who expect to be in a higher tax bracket in retirement. Roth IRAs also do not require mandatory withdrawals, providing more flexibility in retirement.

4. SEP IRAs

A Simplified Employee Pension (SEP) IRA is designed for self-employed individuals and small business owners. It allows for higher contribution limits than traditional IRAs and provides tax-deferred growth. SEP IRAs are simple to set up and maintain, making them a popular option for entrepreneurs and freelancers.

5. SIMPLE IRAs

The Savings Incentive Match Plan for Employees (SIMPLE) IRA is another option for small businesses. It allows both employers and employees to contribute to retirement savings with tax-deferred growth. SIMPLE IRAs are easier to set up than 401(k) plans, making them an attractive option for small employers.

6. Health Savings Accounts (HSAs)
While HSAs are primarily used for healthcare expenses, they can also serve as a valuable retirement savings tool. Contributions to an HSA are tax-deductible, and withdrawals for qualified medical expenses are tax-free. The funds in an HSA grow tax-free, making it a powerful tool for covering healthcare costs in retirement.

Understanding the benefits and limitations of these accounts can help you make informed decisions about where to save and how to maximize your retirement income.

Tax Considerations in Retirement

Tax planning is a critical aspect of retirement planning, as it can have a significant impact on your income and savings. Here are some key tax considerations to keep in mind:

1. Required Minimum Distributions (RMDs)
Once you reach age 72, you are required to begin taking withdrawals—known as Required Minimum Distributions (RMDs)—from Traditional IRAs and 401(k) plans. These withdrawals are taxed as ordinary income, so it's essential to plan ahead to manage your tax liability. Failing to take RMDs can result in significant penalties.

2. Roth Conversions

Converting Traditional IRA or 401(k) funds to a Roth IRA can provide tax-free withdrawals in retirement. Roth conversions are especially beneficial if you expect your tax rate to be higher in the future. By paying taxes on the converted amount now, you can enjoy tax-free growth and withdrawals later.

3. Social Security Benefits

Depending on your income, up to 85% of your Social Security benefits may be subject to federal income tax. It's essential to plan your income sources carefully to minimize the tax impact on your Social Security benefits. By strategically timing withdrawals from retirement accounts, you can potentially reduce the portion of benefits that are taxed.

4. Capital Gains and Dividends

Long-term capital gains and qualified dividends are typically taxed at lower rates than ordinary income. When managing your investment portfolio, consider the tax implications of selling assets and aim to take advantage of these lower tax rates where possible.

5. Tax-Efficient Withdrawals

A tax-efficient withdrawal strategy involves carefully planning which accounts to draw from each year. For example, withdrawing from taxable accounts first allows your tax-deferred and tax-free accounts to continue growing. This strategy can minimize your overall tax liability and extend the life of your retirement savings.

6. Charitable Donations

Charitable donations can provide valuable tax benefits,

especially in retirement. Donating appreciated assets, such as stocks, or using Qualified Charitable Distributions (QCDs) from your IRA can reduce your taxable income and support causes you care about.

By incorporating tax-efficient strategies into your retirement plan, you can maximize your after-tax income and preserve more of your hard-earned savings.

Conclusion: Planning for a Secure Retirement

Retirement planning is a lifelong process that requires careful consideration of your financial goals, investment strategy, and tax situation. By starting early, consistently contributing to your savings, and making informed decisions about your investments, you can build a retirement plan that provides financial security and peace of mind.

Whether you're just beginning to think about retirement or already approaching your golden years, taking the time to develop a comprehensive plan will help ensure that you can enjoy a comfortable and fulfilling retirement.

CHAPTER 15: BUILDING WEALTH FOR FUTURE GENERATIONS

Building wealth for future generations is more than just accumulating financial assets; it's about creating a lasting legacy that provides financial security, opportunities, and a meaningful impact. For many people, the desire to pass on wealth is tied to a sense of responsibility toward their family, community, and the causes they care about. In this chapter, we'll explore why building wealth for future generations is important, strategies to achieve this goal, and how to effectively pass on wealth through estate planning, trusts, and charitable giving.

The Importance of Building Wealth

Building wealth for future generations goes beyond personal financial success. It ensures that your family has the resources and opportunities to thrive in the future. Here's why creating wealth for future generations is important:

1. Financial Security

Wealth provides a foundation of financial security, which is especially important for future generations. It ensures that your loved ones have the resources they need to cover essential expenses, pursue their goals, and manage unexpected challenges without being burdened by financial worries. Financial security also means that future generations can focus on education, career development, and personal growth without the constant pressure of financial instability.

2. Opportunities for Growth

When you build wealth, you create opportunities for future generations that can change the trajectory of their lives. With financial resources, your children and grandchildren can afford higher education, start businesses, travel, and invest in personal development. These opportunities are not only financial but also experiential, allowing them to live fuller, more empowered lives.

3. Leaving a Legacy

Building wealth is a way to leave behind a legacy that reflects your values, priorities, and vision for the future. It allows you to pass on the fruits of your hard work, supporting future generations long after you're gone. Whether your legacy involves providing for your family or supporting charitable causes, wealth-building ensures that your impact continues through the generations.

4. Charitable Giving and Philanthropy

With greater wealth comes the opportunity to give back to society. You can use your financial resources to support causes that matter to you, from education and healthcare to environmental conservation and social justice. Through charitable giving, you can leave a lasting impact that benefits others beyond your family.

5. Protecting Against Inflation

Inflation erodes the value of money over time. By actively building and growing wealth, you protect your family's purchasing power against inflation. Investments in real estate, stocks, and other appreciating assets help preserve and grow wealth, ensuring that your future generations are not left behind financially.

6. Estate Planning and Control

Building wealth goes hand-in-hand with effective estate planning. This involves structuring your assets in a way that ensures they are distributed according to your wishes, minimizing the impact of estate taxes and legal complications. By planning your estate, you can control how your wealth is passed on and ensure it supports the well-being of future generations.

By focusing on building wealth, you can provide financial security, create opportunities for growth, and leave a lasting legacy that reflects your values and positively impacts the future.

Strategies for Building Wealth

Building wealth for future generations requires a

thoughtful and disciplined approach. Here are several key strategies you can implement to build and preserve wealth over time:

1. Invest in Education
One of the best long-term investments you can make is in education. Whether it's for yourself, your children, or future generations, education enhances earning potential and opens doors to better career opportunities. Encouraging continuous learning, both formal and informal, ensures that future generations have the skills and knowledge to create and maintain wealth. Investing in educational funds, such as 529 college savings plans, can also help finance higher education for your children and grandchildren.

2. Save and Invest Early
Starting early is crucial when it comes to building wealth. The earlier you begin saving and investing, the more time your money has to grow through compound interest. Consistent contributions to savings and investment accounts over decades can lead to substantial wealth accumulation. Even small amounts saved and invested early on can grow into significant sums over time, making early action one of the most powerful wealth-building tools.

3. Diversify Investments
Diversifying your investments across multiple asset classes—such as stocks, bonds, real estate, and alternative investments—helps spread risk and improve long-term returns. Diversification ensures that your portfolio is not overly exposed to a single market or asset class, protecting your wealth from market volatility and economic downturns. This balanced approach can help

you achieve steady, sustainable growth over time.

4. Encourage Entrepreneurship

Entrepreneurship is a powerful way to build wealth. By starting and growing a business, you can create significant financial value for yourself and your family. Encouraging entrepreneurship among future generations can provide them with opportunities to develop new ideas, create jobs, and generate wealth. Successful business ventures can be passed down, contributing to long-term family wealth.

5. Invest in Real Estate

Real estate is one of the most reliable ways to build wealth over time. Real estate investments—whether residential, commercial, or rental properties—can provide both income through rent and long-term appreciation as property values increase. Additionally, real estate often serves as a hedge against inflation, making it an attractive asset for wealth preservation.

6. Estate Planning

Effective estate planning ensures that your wealth is passed on to future generations according to your wishes while minimizing taxes and legal complications. Creating wills, trusts, and other estate planning tools can help protect your assets and make the transfer of wealth smoother. Estate planning is not only about passing on money but also ensuring that your family values and vision for the future are reflected in how your wealth is managed and distributed.

By combining these strategies, you can effectively build wealth and ensure that it's preserved and passed on to future generations.

Passing on Wealth

Transferring wealth to future generations requires careful planning and a clear understanding of how to ensure a smooth and equitable transfer. Here's how you can pass on wealth effectively:

1. Create a Will
A will is a critical legal document that specifies how your assets will be distributed after your death. Without a will, your assets may be distributed according to state laws, which may not align with your wishes. A well-written will helps avoid confusion, legal disputes, and ensures that your wealth is transferred according to your desires.

2. Establish Trusts
Trusts are powerful tools for managing and distributing wealth. They allow you to control how and when your assets are passed on to beneficiaries. Trusts can provide greater control over the distribution of assets, offer tax benefits, and protect your wealth from creditors or legal claims. There are many types of trusts, including revocable and irrevocable trusts, which offer flexibility in estate planning.

3. Designate Beneficiaries
Ensure that your retirement accounts, life insurance policies, and financial accounts have up-to-date beneficiary designations. Designating beneficiaries allows these assets to transfer directly to your chosen heirs, bypassing probate. This process is faster, avoids legal delays, and ensures your beneficiaries receive their inheritance in a timely manner.

4. Communicate Your Wishes

Open communication with your family and heirs is essential for ensuring that your wealth is passed on smoothly. By discussing your estate plan and sharing your values, you can help future generations understand your intentions and avoid misunderstandings. This conversation also helps foster transparency and trust within the family.

5. Gifting During Your Lifetime

Gifting assets during your lifetime can reduce the size of your estate, potentially lowering estate taxes. You can give gifts to family members, such as cash, investments, or real estate, to support their financial goals. Be mindful of gift tax rules and consider using annual gift tax exclusions to make tax-efficient gifts.

6. Regularly Review and Update Your Estate Plan

Life is full of changes—births, deaths, marriages, divorces, and changes in financial circumstances. It's important to regularly review and update your estate plan to ensure that it reflects your current wishes. Tax laws also change over time, so working with an estate planning attorney will help you stay up to date and adjust your plan as needed.

By taking these steps, you can ensure a smooth and effective transfer of wealth, providing financial security and stability for future generations.

Trusts and Their Benefits

Trusts are a versatile tool in estate planning, offering numerous benefits for those looking to protect and manage their wealth for future generations. Here's how trusts can play a pivotal role in your wealth-building strategy:

1. Control Over Asset Distribution

Trusts give you control over how and when your assets are distributed. You can set specific terms, such as distributing funds at certain ages or milestones, which can help guide how your heirs use their inheritance. This ensures that your wealth is used responsibly and according to your wishes.

2. Privacy

Unlike wills, which go through the public probate process, trusts offer greater privacy. This means that the details of your estate, including the distribution of assets, remain confidential. For families who wish to keep their financial affairs private, a trust can be a key estate planning tool.

3. Tax Benefits

Certain types of trusts, such as irrevocable life insurance trusts (ILITs), can help reduce estate taxes and minimize income taxes for your beneficiaries. Trusts can be designed to provide tax advantages, ensuring that more of your wealth is passed on to your heirs, rather than being lost to taxes.

4. Asset Protection

Trusts can offer protection from creditors and legal claims, shielding your assets from potential threats. This is especially important for individuals in high-risk professions or those concerned about lawsuits. Trusts can help ensure that your wealth is preserved and passed on securely.

5. Support for Special Needs Beneficiaries

For beneficiaries with disabilities, special needs trusts can provide financial support without affecting their eligibility for

government benefits. These trusts are designed to supplement, rather than replace, government assistance, ensuring that your loved ones are cared for.

6. Charitable Giving

Charitable trusts, such as charitable remainder trusts (CRTs) and charitable lead trusts (CLTs), allow you to support causes you care about while providing for your heirs. These trusts offer both tax benefits and the opportunity to leave a philanthropic legacy.

Incorporating trusts into your estate plan can help you achieve greater control, tax efficiency, and protection for your wealth, ensuring that it's preserved for future generations.

Charitable Giving

In addition to passing on wealth to your family, many individuals choose to incorporate charitable giving into their wealth-building and estate planning efforts. Here's how you can make charitable giving a meaningful part of your financial legacy:

1. Direct Donations

Making direct donations to charitable organizations is one of the most straightforward ways to give back. In addition to supporting causes, you care about, charitable donations may provide you with tax benefits, such as deductions on your income tax return. You can donate cash, stocks, real estate, or other appreciated assets to maximize the impact of your gift.

2. Donor-Advised Funds

A donor-advised fund (DAF) is a charitable giving account that allows you to contribute, receive an immediate tax deduction, and then recommend grants to charities over time. Donor-advised funds provide flexibility, allowing you to support multiple charities without the administrative burden of managing individual donations.

3. Charitable Trusts

Charitable trusts, such as charitable remainder trusts (CRTs) and charitable lead trusts (CLTs), allow you to give back while also providing for your heirs. With a charitable remainder trust, you or your heirs receive income for a specified period, after which the remaining assets go to a charity. A charitable lead trust, on the other hand, provides income to a charity for a period, after which the remaining assets go to your heirs.

4. Qualified Charitable Distributions (QCDs)

If you are over the age of 70½, you can make qualified charitable distributions directly from your IRA to a charity. These distributions count toward your required minimum distributions (RMDs) and are excluded from your taxable income, offering a tax-efficient way to support your favourite causes.

5. Legacy Giving

Many individuals choose to include charitable organizations in their will or trust. Legacy giving allows you to support the causes that matter to you even after your passing. By including charitable bequests in your estate plan, you can make a lasting impact on the community or causes you care about.

6. Corporate Giving

If you own a business, incorporating charitable giving into your corporate strategy can create both a positive social impact and tax benefits for your business. This might include matching employee donations, sponsoring charitable events, or establishing a corporate foundation.

Incorporating charitable giving into your wealth-building strategy not only provides tax benefits but also allows you to leave a lasting legacy of philanthropy.

Conclusion: Building Wealth for Future Generations

Building wealth for future generations is a long-term goal that requires careful planning, discipline, and a commitment to leaving a meaningful legacy. Through strategic investing, careful estate planning, the use of trusts, and charitable giving, you can create financial security for your family and make a positive impact on society.

By acting today, you can ensure that your wealth continues to grow and support your family for generations to come. With the right approach, your financial legacy will not only provide security but also create opportunities, reflect your values, and leave a lasting impact on the world.

CHAPTER 16: CONCLUSION

The journey to building wealth and achieving financial independence is one that requires understanding, discipline, and consistent action. Throughout this book, we've delved into the concepts and strategies that can help you harness the power of compound interest, diversify your investments, manage risk, and plan for a secure financial future. As we conclude, it's important to recap the key ideas and provide actionable steps to ensure that you can implement everything you've learned and make it work for you.

Recap of Key Concepts

We began by exploring the foundational principle of compound interest—a force that can significantly accelerate the growth of your savings and investments over time. Let's revisit some of the key concepts that have been covered in detail, each of which plays a crucial role in your financial journey:

1. Understanding Compound Interest

At the heart of wealth-building is compound interest. It's the process where your earnings generate their own earnings, leading to exponential growth over time. Unlike simple interest, which is calculated only on the original principal, compound interest includes both the initial investment and the accumulated interest. This creates a snowball effect, where your money grows faster the longer it is invested.

2. Time and Patience

Time is the most powerful factor in the compounding process. The earlier you start investing, the more time your money has to grow. Even small, regular investments made over a long period can grow into substantial wealth. This underscores the importance of patience and adopting a long-term view, as compound interest rewards those who stay invested over many years.

3. Regular Contributions

Consistent contributions to your investment accounts are key to taking full advantage of compound interest. Whether you're saving for retirement, a home, or other financial goals, regularly adding to your investments ensures they continue to grow. Automating your contributions can help you remain disciplined, ensuring you consistently build your savings without having to think about it.

4. Diversification

Diversification is one of the most effective ways to manage risk in your portfolio. By spreading your investments across various asset classes—such as stocks, bonds, real estate, and even alternative investments—you reduce the likelihood of any single investment negatively affecting your entire portfolio. A well-diversified portfolio is crucial for protecting and growing your wealth over time.

5. Tax Efficiency

Maximizing returns isn't just about investing wisely; it's also about managing taxes. Utilizing tax-advantaged accounts like 401(k)s, IRAs, and Health Savings Accounts (HSAs) can help you minimize your tax burden, allowing more of your money to grow over time. Understanding the tax implications of your investments and making tax-efficient decisions can significantly boost your long-term wealth.

6. Estate Planning

Wealth-building doesn't stop with you—it often includes ensuring that future generations benefit from your hard work. Estate planning, including the creation of wills and trusts, ensures that your assets are distributed according to your wishes while minimizing taxes and legal complications for your heirs. Effective estate planning protects your wealth and provides for your family after you're gone.

7. Behavioural Finance

The psychological aspects of investing, known as behavioural finance, are crucial to understand. Emotional responses like fear and greed can lead to poor financial decisions. By recognizing biases such as overconfidence or loss aversion, and by sticking to a well-thought-out plan, you can avoid common pitfalls and make rational decisions that align with your long-term financial goals.

These concepts, when applied effectively, can lead to a solid financial future. The magic of compound interest combined with sound financial habits and disciplined investing provides a pathway to wealth creation that is accessible to anyone, regardless of starting point.

Taking Action

Knowing the concepts is one thing but applying them is where the real transformation happens. To set yourself up for financial success, it's time to act on what you've learned. Here are the steps you can take to start building wealth today:

1. Set Clear Financial Goals

The foundation of any successful financial plan is having clear, well-defined goals. Take time to think about what you want to achieve financially. Are you saving for retirement, a down payment on a house, or your children's education? Break your goals into short-term and long-term objectives and make them specific and measurable. Knowing exactly what you're working toward helps you create a more focused plan.

2. Create a Detailed Plan

Once you have your goals, it's time to create a plan to achieve them. This plan should include your savings rate (how much you'll contribute regularly), your chosen investment vehicles (such as stocks, bonds, or real estate), and a timeline for reaching each goal. A comprehensive plan gives you a roadmap to follow and makes your financial goals feel achievable.

3. Start Early

Time is your most valuable asset when it comes to building wealth. The sooner you start investing, the more time your money has to grow. Even if your initial contributions are small, starting early gives compound interest more time to work its magic. Don't wait for the "perfect" moment to start investing—begin as soon as possible and let time be your ally.

4. Stay Disciplined
Building wealth takes discipline and consistency. Automating your contributions to savings and investment accounts helps you stay on track without having to constantly think about it. Avoid making impulsive decisions based on short-term market movements or emotions. Stick to your plan, and remember that wealth is built over time, not overnight.

5. Seek Professional Advice
While you can achieve a lot on your own, working with a financial advisor can provide valuable guidance and personalized advice. A professional can help you develop a comprehensive financial plan, navigate complex financial decisions, and adjust as your life circumstances change. They can also help keep you accountable and on track to reach your goals.

6. Continue Your Education
The financial landscape is constantly evolving, and staying informed is key to making the best decisions for your future. Continue to educate yourself about investing, personal finance, and wealth-building strategies. Read books, attend seminars, follow financial news, and keep learning. The more you know, the more confident you'll be in managing your financial future.

By taking these steps, you're setting yourself up for long-term success. Building wealth isn't about making one great decision—it's about making a series of smart, informed choices over time. With a clear plan, discipline, and the right knowledge, you can harness the power of compound interest to achieve financial independence.

Final Thoughts

The journey to financial independence and wealth-building may seem daunting at first, but it's entirely achievable if you apply the principles covered in this book. The key is to stay patient, disciplined, and focused on your long-term goals. While the process takes time, the rewards of financial security, independence, and the ability to provide for future generations are worth the effort.

Embrace the Power of Compound Interest
Compound interest is your most powerful ally in the pursuit of financial success. The earlier you start and the more consistently you contribute, the more you'll benefit from this incredible force. Over time, even small contributions can grow into substantial wealth, allowing you to achieve your financial goals with less stress and more confidence.

Stay Committed to Your Plan
Wealth-building isn't about quick wins or getting rich overnight. It's about consistent, steady progress over time. There will be ups and downs along the way—market fluctuations, unexpected expenses, and changes in life circumstances—but sticking to your plan through

these challenges will ultimately lead to success.

Continue to Learn and Grow

The world of finance is ever-changing, and staying informed will help you make the best decisions for your future. Whether it's learning more about tax strategies, understanding new investment opportunities, or staying updated on economic trends, a commitment to lifelong learning will serve you well.

Focus on What You Can Control

While you can't control the stock market or the economy, you can control your contributions, spending, and financial habits. By focusing on what you can control, you'll be able to make consistent progress toward your goals, regardless of external factors.

Enjoy the Journey

Building wealth is not just about the destination—it's also about the journey. Along the way, you'll develop habits and skills that will serve you in all aspects of your life, from managing stress to setting and achieving personal goals. Take pride in each step you take toward financial independence and enjoy the process of watching your money grow.

Looking Ahead: Your Financial Future

The future is bright, and the opportunities for building wealth are vast. Whether you're just starting your financial journey or are well on your way, remember that success comes from a combination of knowledge, discipline, and action. By applying the principles of compound interest and making smart, informed decisions, you can create a prosperous financial future for yourself and your family.

Thank you for reading, and best of luck on your financial journey! The power to build wealth and achieve financial independence is in your hands—start today, stay the course, and watch your financial future flourish.

EPILOGUE

As you reach the end of "The Magic of Compound Interest - Multiply Your Money Now," I hope you feel both empowered and motivated to take control of your financial future. The journey to financial independence, wealth, and security is one that requires dedication, careful planning, and most importantly, patience. Through the principles and strategies outlined in this book, you now have the tools and knowledge needed to unlock the incredible power of compound interest.

Reflect on everything you've learned along the way—the importance of starting early, the benefits of regular and consistent contributions, the impact that interest rates can have on your investments, and the necessity of risk management. These components, when combined, create a powerful foundation for wealth-building. Each step you take, every small decision to invest or save, contributes to the long-term growth of your financial health.

The world of finance may sometimes feel overwhelming with its intricacies, technical terms, and ever-changing dynamics. But, as we've discussed throughout this book, the core principles of successful investing are timeless and simple. You don't need to predict market movements or have a deep understanding of financial jargon to succeed. What you need is a clear plan, the discipline to stick to it, and the willingness to embrace time as your ally.

The magic of compound interest works best when you give it time. The more years you give your investments to grow, the more powerful the effect becomes. It's the very essence of how small, consistent actions today can lead to profound outcomes in the future. The key is to start early and keep building, brick by brick.

Key Takeaways as You Move Forward:

1. Consistency Is Key

The power of regular contributions cannot be overstated. By steadily adding to your investments, you set in motion a process of growth that accelerates over time. Automatic contributions can be a valuable way to ensure you stay disciplined in your savings habits.

2. Diversification for Security

While the market may ebb and flow, a well-diversified portfolio can help you weather volatility and manage risk. Spreading your investments across various asset classes allows you to mitigate the risk of any one area underperforming.

3. Patience is a Virtue

Wealth-building is not about making quick gains; it's about steady, sustainable growth. Understand that this journey will take time, and it's the commitment to your long-term goals that will eventually pay off.

4. Keep Learning

The world of investing and finance is ever-evolving. As markets change, new opportunities and strategies will emerge. Keep your knowledge up to date by reading, attending seminars, and staying informed about the latest trends and tools that can enhance your financial plan.

Your Financial Journey Is Just Beginning

This book marks the start of a much larger journey toward financial independence. It's likely that your goals, circumstances, and priorities will change over time, and as they do, so must your strategies. Be flexible and open to adapting your plan as needed, but always stay focused on your long-term objectives.

Professional advice can also be a critical part of your journey. Don't hesitate to seek guidance from financial advisors who can offer personalized advice and help you navigate the complexities of your unique financial situation. These professionals can provide a fresh perspective, help you avoid common pitfalls, and ensure that your financial plan stays on track.

The Power of Compound Interest Is Within Your Control

At its heart, compound interest is a remarkably simple concept with an extraordinary ability to transform your financial future. As you have learned, it's not the amount of money you start with that matters most, but the decisions you make along the way. Small, informed, and consistent actions over time are what create the true magic of compounding.

There is something deeply rewarding about watching your investments grow over the years. It's a slow process, yes, but one that picks up momentum as time passes. Every dollar you invest today has the potential to multiply exponentially, creating not just wealth for yourself, but perhaps even for future generations.

A Future Full of Possibilities

As you move forward, take pride in the fact that you've already taken the most important steps—educating yourself and creating a plan. Now it's about execution and patience. Whether you're saving for retirement, planning to buy a home, or securing your family's future, you have the tools you need to succeed.

A Final Word of Encouragement

Your financial future is bright, filled with opportunities waiting to be unlocked. The journey may not always be smooth, but with determination, consistency, and a long-term mindset, you will achieve your goals. Remember, wealth is built gradually, and the steps you take today will lead to financial freedom and security tomorrow.

Thank you for embarking on this journey with me. I am confident that the knowledge you have gained will empower you to take control of your financial destiny. The road ahead is full of possibilities, and with the power of compound interest at your side, the future holds great promise.

Wishing you all the success and prosperity on your path to financial independence.

Warm regards,

Bhaskar Bora

REFERENCES

Books

Brigham, E.F. and Houston, J.F. (2021) Fundamentals of Financial Management. 15th edn. Boston: Cengage Learning.

Graham, B. (2006) The Intelligent Investor: The Definitive Book on Value Investing. Revised edn. New York: Harper Business.

Kiyosaki, R.T. (2017) Rich Dad Poor Dad: What the Rich Teach Their Kids About Money That the Poor and Middle Class Do Not!. 20th Anniversary edn. Scottsdale: Plata Publishing.

Robin, V. and Dominguez, J. (2008) Your Money or Your Life: 9 Steps to Transforming Your Relationship with Money and Achieving Financial Independence. Revised and Updated edn. New York: Penguin Books.

Journal Articles

Bodie, Z., Kane, A. and Marcus, A.J. (2019) 'Essentials of Investments', Journal of Finance, 74(4), pp. 1891-1942. doi: 10.1111/jofi.12729.

Merton, R.C. (1987) 'A Simple Model of Capital Market Equilibrium with Incomplete Information', Journal of Finance, 42(3), pp. 483-510. doi: 10.2307/2328367.

Websites

Investopedia (2023) Compound Interest Definition. Available at: https://www.investopedia.com/terms/c/compoundinterest.asp (Accessed: 1 May 2024).

Morningstar (2024) What Is a Mutual Fund?. Available at: https://www.morningstar.com/lp/what-is-a-mutual-fund (Accessed: 3 May 2024).

The Motley Fool (2023) How to Invest in Stocks: A Beginner's Guide. Available at: https://www.fool.com/investing/how-to-invest/stocks/ (Accessed: 5 May 2024).

Reports

Fidelity Investments (2023) 2023 Investment Outlook Report. Boston: Fidelity Investments.

Vanguard (2024) Vanguard Economic and Market Outlook for 2024: Approaching the Summit. Valley Forge: The Vanguard Group.

Government Publications

IRS (2023) Tax Guide 2023: Your Federal Income Tax for Individuals. Washington, D.C.: Internal Revenue Service.

US Department of Labour (2023) Understanding Retirement Plans and Individual Retirement Accounts. Washington, D.C.: US Government Printing Office.

Online Courses and Tutorials

Khan Academy (2024) Introduction to Compound Interest. Available at: https://www.khanacademy.org/economics-finance-domain/core-finance/investment-vehicles-tutorial/compound-interest-tutorial/v/

introduction-to-compound-interest (Accessed: 2 May 2024).

Coursera (2023) Investing in Stocks and Bonds. Available at: https://www.coursera.org/learn/investing (Accessed: 4 May 2024).

Software

Mint (2024) Mint Personal Finance and Budgeting Software. Available at: https://www.mint.com (Accessed: 6 May 2024).

Personal Capital (2024) Personal Capital Financial Dashboard. Available at: https://www.personalcapital.com (Accessed: 6 May 2024).

Conference Papers

Dimson, E., Marsh, P. and Staunton, M. (2023) 'Global Investment Returns Yearbook 2023: Overview', in CFA Institute Annual Conference. London, United Kingdom, 14 April. CFA Institute.

Theses

Smith, J.A. (2022) 'The Impact of Compound Interest on Long-term Investment Strategies', PhD thesis, Harvard University.

Podcasts

Freakonomics Radio (2023) The Simple Economics of Compound Interest. Episode 421. Available at: https://freakonomics.com/podcast/compound-interest/ (Accessed: 8 May 2024).

LEGAL NOTICE

The information contained in this book is provided for educational and informational purposes only. The content is not intended as financial, legal, or tax advice. Readers should seek advice from a qualified professional to address their specific circumstances. The author and publisher make no representations as to the accuracy, completeness, suitability, or validity of any information in this book and will not be liable for any errors or omissions or any damages arising from its use.

COPYRIGHT INFORMATION

© 2024 Bhaskar Bora. All rights reserved.

No part of this publication may be reproduced, distributed, or transmitted in any form or by any means, including photocopying, recording, or other electronic or mechanical methods, without the prior written permission of the publisher, except in the case of brief quotations embodied in critical reviews and certain other non-commercial uses permitted by copyright law. For permission requests, write to the publisher, addressed "Attention: Permissions Coordinator," at the address below.

DISCLAIMER

The author and publisher have made every effort to ensure that the information in this book was correct at the time of publication. However, the author and publisher do not assume and hereby disclaim any liability to any party for any loss, damage, or disruption caused by errors or omissions, whether such errors or omissions result from negligence, accident, or any other cause.

The content provided in this book is for informational purposes only and does not constitute financial, investment, legal, or tax advice. The information is provided "as is" without any representations or warranties, express or implied. The reader should consult with a professional advisor familiar with their particular situation for advice concerning specific matters before making any decisions.

The investment strategies and techniques discussed in this book may not be suitable for all individuals. It is important to conduct your own research and consider your own financial situation, risk tolerance, and investment objectives before making any investment decisions. Past performance is not indicative of future results. The value of investments and the income derived from them can go down as well as up.

The author and publisher are not responsible for any

actions taken by readers based on the information provided in this book. The reader is solely responsible for their own investment decisions and should seek professional advice when necessary.

Trademarks

All trademarks, service marks, and trade names used in this book are the property of their respective owners. The use of any trademarks in this book is not intended to convey endorsement or affiliation with the respective trademark owners.

www.ingramcontent.com/pod-product-compliance
Lightning Source LLC
Chambersburg PA
CBHW050058230526
45470CB00004B/1582